Silke Pfersdorf

101 Design Classics

1920 until today

teNeues

CONTENT

101 Design Classics

Foreword	8
Ball Clock (George Nelson | 1948)	10
Componibili (Anna Castelli Ferrieri | 1967)	12
Cabbage Chair (Oki Sato | 2008)	14
Tea Trolley 901 (Alvar Aalto | 1936)	16
Gräshoppa (Greta Grossman | 1947)	18
Loop Chair (Willy Guhl | 1954)	20
Tac 01 (Walter Gropius | 1969)	24
Tolix Stool (Xavier Pauchard | 1934)	28
Melt (Tom Dixon | 2015)	30
Lido (Battista and Gino Giudici | 1936)	34
Monkey (Jaime Hayon | 2010)	36
Unikko (Maija Isola | 1964)	38
Wishbone Chair (Hans J. Wegner | 1949)	40
Sciangai (De Pas, D'Urbino and Lomazzi | 1973)	42
Oda (Sebastian Herkner | 2014)	44
Monkey (Kay Bojesen | 1951)	46
AB 1 Alarm Clock (Dieter Rams and Dietrich Lubs | 1987)	50
Zettel'z (Ingo Maurer | 1997)	52
Stelton EM77 (Eric Magnussen | 1977)	54
Acapulco Chair („Mr. X" | 1950s)	58
Kaiser Idell 6631 (Christian Dell | 1933)	60
Bocca (Studio 65 | 1970)	62
Bolle (Tapio Wirkkala | 1966)	66
Ball Chair (Eero Aarnio | 1963)	68
Araignée (Serge Mouille | 1951)	70
Poeten (Finn Juhl | 1941)	74
Luxembourg Chair (Paris Parks Department | 1923)	76
Kubus (Mogens Lassen | 1962)	78
Altorfer Deck Chair (Huldreich Altorfer jr. | 1948)	80
La Cupola (Aldo Rossi | 1989)	82
Marshmallow Sofa (George Nelson | 1956)	84
Snoopy (Achille and Pier Giacomo Castiglioni | 1967)	86
Superleggera (Giovanni Ponti | 1951)	88
Uno, la mela (Enzo Mari | 1963)	90
Lounge Chair (Charles and Ray Eames | 1956)	92
Tema e Variazioni (Piero Fornasetti | 1950s)	96
Air (Marcus Engman | 1980s)	98
Molar Stool (Philipp Mainzer | 1996)	100
USM Haller (Fritz Haller | 1963)	102
Knotted Chair (Marcel Wanders | 1996)	106
String Shelf (Kajsa and Nils „Nisse" Strinning | 1949)	108
Barcelona Chair (Lilly Reich and Ludwig Mies van der Rohe | 1996)	110
E1 Desk (Egon Eiermann | 1953)	114
Plastic Chair (Charles und Ray Eames | 1950)	118
Billy (Gillis Lundgren | 1978)	120
Juicy Salif (Philippe Starck | 1990)	122
Artichoke (Poul Henningsen | 1958)	124
Tulip Table (Eero Saarinen | 1957)	128
Lamy 2000 (Gerd A. Müller | 1966)	130
KitchenAid (Herbert Johnston | 1927)	132
Uten.Silo (Dorothee Becker | 1968)	136
Shuffle Table MH1 (Mia Hamborg | 2010)	138

SD (Stefan Diez | 2016)	140	**Butterfly** (Sori Yanagi | 1954)	212
Le Creuset Cookware (Armand Desaegher and Octave Aubecq | 1925)	142	**Maly Bed** (Peter Maly | 1983)	216
Laccio (Marcel Breuer | 1925)	144	**Blow** (De Pas, D'Urbino, Lomazzi and Scolari | 1967)	218
FlowerPot (Verner Panton | 1968)	146	**Toucan** (Enea Ferrari | 1964)	220
Plumy (Annie Hiéronimus | 1980)	148	**Lyngby Vase** (Lyngby Porcelæn | 1930er-Jahre)	222
Stendig (Massimo Vignelli | 1966)	150	**S 33** (Mart Stam | 1926)	224
Tube Light (Eileen Gray | 1927)	154	**Nesting Tables** (Josef Albers | 1926)	226
Antibodi (Patricia Urquiola | 2006)	156	**Parupu** (Claesson Koivisto Rune | 2009)	228
Coffee Table (Isamu Noguchi | 1947)	160	**Wristwatch** (Max Bill | 1961)	230
Elephant (Charles and Ray Eames | 1945)	162	**The Tired Man** (Flemming Lassen | 1935)	232
G-type (Masahiro Mori | 1958)	166	**Frankfurt Kitchen** (Margarete Schütte-Lihotzky | 1926)	236
Vipp (Holger Nielsen | 1939)	168	**Sacco** (Gatti, Paolini und Teodoro | 1968)	240
Z.Stuhl (Ernst Moeckl | 1973)	172	**Ulm Stool** (Max Bill | 1954)	242
Flamingo (Michele de Lucchi | 1984)	176	**Pirandello** (Jasper Morrison | 2013)	244
FNP (Axel Kufus | 1989)	178	**Palissade** (Erwan and Ronan Bouroullec | 2015)	246
FK 6725 (Preben Fabricius and Jørgen Kastholm | 1964)	182	**Polder** (Hella Jongerius | 2015)	250
Rupfentiere (Renate Müller | 1967)	184	**Tableware 137** (Hedwig Bollhagen | 1955)	252
Siesta Chair (Ingmar Relling | 1965)	188	**2002** (Christian Werner | 2015)	254
Hot Bertaa (Philippe Starck | 1985)	192	**Mono Zeug** (Michael Schneider | 1995)	256
Waves (Alvar Aalto | 1937)	194	**Vespa** (Corradino D'Ascanio | 1946)	258
Egg Chair (Arne Jacobsen | 1958)	196	**Fleeze** (Winfried Totzek | 1988)	260
Bookworm (Ron Arad | 1994)	200	**Big Easy Chair** (Ron Arad | 1988)	264
LC4 Chaise Longue (Charlotte Perriand | 1928)	202		
Apple iMac (Jonathan Ive | 1997)	204		
Design Letters (Arne Jacobsen | 1961)	206	Index	266
Antelope Chair (Ernest Race | 1951)	208	Picture Credits	270
Pompidou (Jonathan Adler | 2012)	210	The Author	271

Foreword

The English say you should never judge a book by its cover. By this they mean that things are not always what they seem, that sometimes the truth does not present itself as plainly as you might like. This saying also applies to things labeled as "design." The term design seems to be on everyone's lips, and its inflationary use cannot even be construed as a disadvantage. It seems like anything can claim to be a design object—any unsuccessful cabinet, any misshapen lamp, any little table, no matter how ill-proportioned—after all, someone had to dream up the shape. Linguistically speaking, design is a direct descendant of the Italian "disegno," which originally meant a drawing, an idea, a sketch. Nothing more. So whether we like it or not, we are surrounded by design every day. It is impossible to escape and certainly impossible to overlook. That's perfectly fine, and you can live with it—as long as you recognize that this little word is far from being an aristocratic title. Even if it is increasingly being treated as such these days.

The same holds true for the "classics." There is no authority that sets binding standards or even a rule of thumb according to which a piece of furniture rises to be hailed as a classic after, say, ten or twenty years. After all, it is ultimately about the influence it has on culture, the timelessness that surrounds it, and its name recognition.

So with the title of our book, some might argue that we are skidding across a patch of black ice even though, as we all know, there is always a clear line to follow. In fact, it was not always easy to select the 101 pieces we feature in this book. Some decisions were fiercely contested, and at times personal taste battled desperately with the recognition that one or the other piece of furniture or accessory had earned in the eyes of society—and in the end had to admit defeat. Our best-of selection is not based on a whim or a mood—and yet it remains highly subjective. And we freely admit it: The century has produced an unbelievable number of icons who weren't even mentioned in passing. Our line-up is made up of more than just winners; we had losers in our ranks as well. You can learn a lot from failure, and sometimes a false start explains the principle of success better than the winner itself.

A lackluster introduction to the pieces? Boring.

A lackluster introduction to the pieces? Boring. In this book you'll find stories about design and designers, classifications, comparisons, and reflections. All the things that bring objects to life. That leaves the unavoidable warning about side effects: If one or the other of these pieces of furniture catches your eye, it may prove to be expensive. Design can do many things, but rarely cheaply.

So leaf through, read, marvel—and most importantly, have fun! Because that is the most precious quality of good design pieces: They make life sweeter, funnier, and more beautiful.

Never judge a book by its cover? This one looks pretty good to me. And its contents will not disappoint you either.

George Nelson | 1948

Ball Clock

Let's slow down and take it easy. But that's easier said than done when time is racing. When it is breathing down our necks, is getting tight, or running out. It makes us slaves, rushes us through life, and causes us to despair over our full appointment calendars. Hasn't the most important task of our everyday lives long been to keep an eye on the clock? Which doesn't exactly make it any more popular as a means of applying pressure. In Hollywood movies, it becomes a symbol for a lousy start to the day, with the protagonist banging on the merciless alarm clock while still half asleep. As an attractive accessory gracing your arm, at least the wristwatch makes a good impression.

Unfortunately, trying to be on time no longer passes for the gold standard of personal optimization—which is why we are increasingly strapping on offshoots of our smartphones that count steps and monitor calories, heart rate, and vitamin intake. Perhaps it would be better if we kept clocks at a distance. A few meters at least, between us and an hour display on the wall. Unfortunately, those who keep up with the times often forgo hands, and instead translate the hours and minutes into words or use a projector to make them glow digitally above the sofa. No offense intended to any of these variations, but sometimes timelessness is not the worst quality for a clock.

If you're looking for truly enduring values that have been almost unaffected by the passing of the decades, you'll soon encounter George Nelson's Ball Clock. In 1947, after a night of drinking with friends, Nelson supposedly found an initial cursory sketch of the clock while gathering up papers filled with scribbles that had been scattered around his apartment. Nelson didn't remember anything, and apparently neither did anyone else, so he and his designer buddy Irving Harper just kept trying out different sketches of it.

"The Ball Clock incorporates Nelson's idea that you don't need numbers to tell the time," says Nelson expert Jochen Eisenbrand, chief curator of the Vitra Design Museum. The position of the hands is enough for you to recognize at a glance what time it is. With such simplification, Nelson, who was 40 years old at the time, was clearly ahead of his time. In other respects, the clock with its twelve colorful spheres was perfectly suited to an era that, after the gray years of World War II, longed for the colorfulness of life. For Nelson, the Ball Clock marked the beginning of an amazing series, which resulted in more than 150 wall clock models that he and his colleagues from George Nelson Associates designed for the Howard Miller Clock Company. Most of these models are reminiscent of suns or stars—things with a thoroughly positive connotation. What can we learn from the Ball Clock? That the hours of the day should be filled with color. That every day is another chance to stay on the ball. Or that there is always time to take it easy.

A magnificent timepiece: Newly reissued by Vitra, the legendary Ball Clock is available in numerous versions.

01

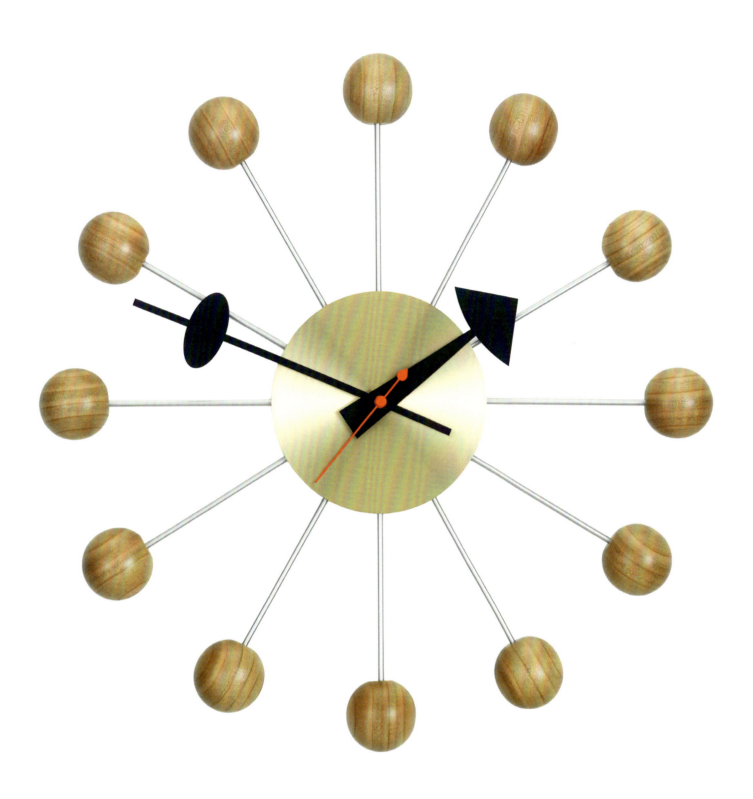

Daniel Radcliffe has a problem: Harry Potter. In the movies he battled the dark Lord Voldemort, while in real life he has battled his alter ego: the young wizard with the jagged scar on his forehead. His name appears to be eternally linked to his role. It's a problem that some of his colleagues have experienced as well: Angelina Jolie is haunted by Lara Croft, Daniel Craig by James Bond. And Diane Keaton is somehow always the woman you can rely on.

Even furniture can suffer from image issues; some pieces are divas and automatically capture the starring role in any room. Others, on the other hand, attract attention only after a second look and are thus automatically relegated to the supporting role. There are also pieces doomed to stand in the corner for eternity, useful but rather unimpressive. And then there is the Componibili, which stands somewhere between the chairs. It is a position, by the way, that has always proved to be an excellent one for it. In the history of design, there has probably never been a piece of furniture that, over the course of time, has made it into every corner of every house all over the world, from the living room to the bedroom to the kitchen and bathroom. In filmmaking, this excellent characteristic would be called versatile and changeable. The Componibili could be a bedside table, a minibar, a writing desk, or even be planted with houseplants without complaint. Lorenza Luti, granddaughter of its inventor Anna Castelli Ferrieri, recalls that every room in her grandmother's house had one of these pieces—each in a different color.

Anna Castelli Ferrieri | 1967

Componibili

Architect Castelli Ferrieri was actually an urban planner—but by designing the colorful container, in a sense she shifted her job from the big to the small: It created (storage) space where it was needed.

This little jack-of-all-trades never made much of a fuss about itself, but over the decades it rolled straight into the ranks of the legends. Speaking of legends: The first Componibili was actually originally a square design, good and practical. It was the round shape, however, that helped it achieve a breakthrough—which prompted Castelli Ferrieri to give the story a little, well, nuance. The Componibili had already been a success, she later claimed, when she and her husband had founded the Kartell furniture company, where their baby is still being made. Even if their offspring is more of a girl-next-door character than a diva, it has still copied the airs and graces of many celebrity women: It has somehow kept its exact age a secret. The annals of design contain a wide variety of birth dates, but it was probably sometime towards the end of the 1960s that it was born. Nevertheless, true grandeur is ageless.

02

Top: The inventor Anna Castelli Ferrieri—she created space where it was needed.

Below: Componibili—versatile, changeable, an all-round success, so to say.

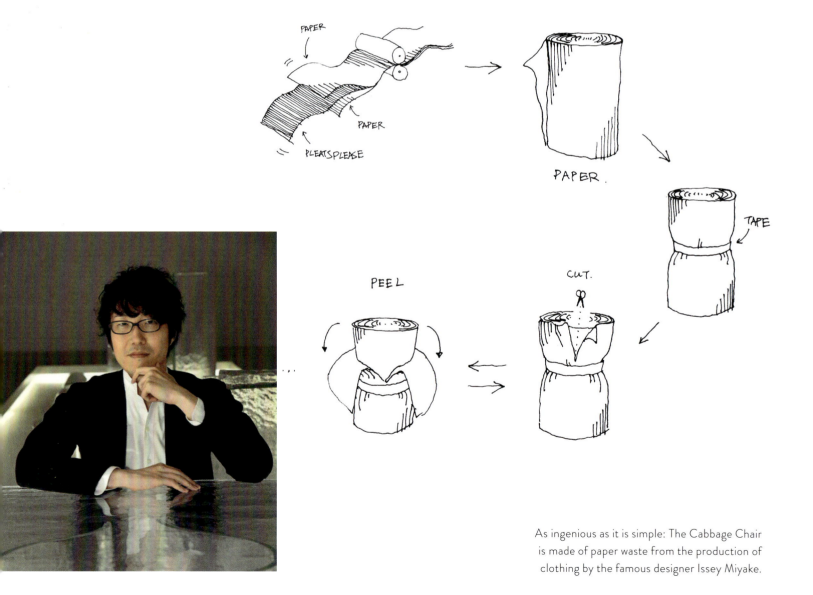

As ingenious as it is simple: The Cabbage Chair is made of paper waste from the production of clothing by the famous designer Issey Miyake.

03

Oki Sato | 2008

Cabbage Chair

There is still much to learn even as a great designer, and sometimes this is how a single piece of furniture becomes the greatest teacher of all. Oki Sato founded the label Nendo (Japanese for "dough") with friends in a garage in 2002. Yet it was the commission from famous fashion designer Issey Miyake in 2007 that taught him an important lesson. He was tasked with designing an armchair for the Japanese fashion star. Miyake asked that Sato use the waste by-product created during the production of his pleated fabric: vast quantities of paper deposited between the flattened layers of fabric. After using several full chemical baths to strengthen the paper, Sato tinkered with a prototype. It was his first try, but Miyake was thrilled: "That's it!" he exclaimed, forbidding him to improve the piece any further. Yet Sato viewed it as a work in progress and thus still in its infancy. He hesitated at first, but then realized that perhaps sometimes it's better to end a sentence even if you think there's more to be said. Not an easy task for someone who is convinced that there are always two ways to reach a goal: one easy and one difficult. The easy path leads straight to the result, while the more difficult one meanders, leads over obstacles, and sometimes even straight into a dead end. But in the end, it takes you further.

To come to this conclusion about wrapping things up, Sato probably had to simply take a leap of faith. When it comes to starting a new design adventure, however, his early rules still apply, such as the following: Only in the beginning is an idea as fresh as sashimi, the Toronto-born Japanese designer is convinced. That's why he doesn't spend a lot of time discussing his ideas with others at first, and he doesn't constantly toss them back and forth like a steak in a frying pan, to stick with the food analogy. It's easy to imagine that thoughts must race around in his head like cooks in a large kitchen—after all, his three studios in Tokyo, Milan, and Shanghai are sometimes working on as many as 400 projects at the same time, and he himself has stated that he has nothing but design on his mind 24/7. Who knows whether Doraemon—a cat-like robot cartoon character who is as famous in Japan as Mickey Mouse—serves as his role model? Sato himself, however, has affirmed that Doraemon's adventures are his favorite manga. In the series, Doraemon uses gadgets from the future to help a little boy named Nobita out of trouble. With lots of things that make everyday life easier and better. It sounds like a noble task... and somehow also a bit like Sato. Sato still demands that most of his designs have that certain something extra, a playful, witty touch, despite all the minimalism. It seems like Doraemon has definitely made things easier for himself.

04

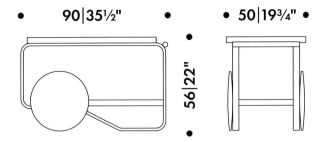

Alvar Aalto | 1936

Tea Trolley 901

A distance of 8,650 kilometers is a long way. And yet this is at least how far Scandinavia and Japan lie apart from each other. They are even worlds apart, you might say. But if you were to thumb through lifestyle magazines from both countries, you might wonder whether the far north and the distant east are in fact bound together by a magical ribbon. Whether they are congenial partners or kindred spirits, the two regions have uncannily similar styles: clean lines and a predilection for natural materials and good craftsmanship. Nevertheless, they do also have certain differences. The Japanese sibling is more refined and highly disciplined, her Scandinavian sister more relaxed and rustic. So instead of talking about family ties, perhaps we should recognize their shared preferences and the inspiration they draw from each other, ultimately resulting in fruitful tête-à-têtes between the creatives from the individual nations. Which also sometimes led to design sponsorships. Muji, the Japanese retail chain, stocked its shelves with Swedish-inspired products under the name Muji Sweden. Conversely, the Danmark design museum in Copenhagen mounted a major exhibition called *Learning From Japan*, which demonstrated the Japanese influence on local designers since 1870. In geographic terms, this influence was far broader, of course. Indeed, it extending all the way to Finland, for instance, where the famous architect Alvar Aalto lived with his wife Aino. Finland was also home to the Ishikawas, a married couple attached to the Japanese embassy, who cultivated Aalto's growing enthusiasm for Nippon architecture and fine woodwork. The Japanese, he felt, lent wood a certain elegance in all things big and small. Aalto discovered prime examples in Stockholm, including the delightful Zui-Ki-Tei teahouse, with which the Japanese honored the city in 1935. An admiring Aalto visited it every couple of months. Although this influence can be clearly seen in his architecture, Aalto's smaller designs also reflect the Japanese elegance he held in such high regard. One example is the Tea Trolley 901, designed in 1936, which has since rolled through living rooms all over the world. For die-hard coffee drinkers like the Finns, this borders on treason. Statistics show that, thanks to a regular habit of coffee breaks, Finland's per capita consumption is one liter per day in, breaking every world record. However, if you think Aalto's tea trolley draws a straight line to Japan and its tea ceremony, you might want to reconsider. Alvar and his wife Aino took a rather classic approach and were more likely to be found enjoying British tea than imbibing a green matcha.

Dutch designer Hella Jongerius has since updated Aalto's tea cart with a version made from dark wood and a tray in deep aubergine. Another stylish design. And yet the zeitgeist has now come up with a way to describe Nordic design with Japanese stylistic elements: japandi. An arranged marriage between Japan and Scandinavia. And what happens when you add the Netherlands to the mix? Whatever you call it, the result is a vibrant threesome.

Greta Grossman | 1947

Gräshoppa

The name Gräshoppa sounds a little like something you'd on the shelves of a big-box furniture store, but that's always the case when you put Swedish labels on mass-market interior accessories. And yet the lamp designed by Greta Grossman came not from the frozen north, but from sunny California. At the start of the 1940s, the interior designer and her husband, American jazz musician Billy Grossman, moved to Los Angeles, where Greta saw to it that stars like Ingrid Bergman and Greta Garbo had beautiful and comfortable homes. It was a lucrative business, especially since Swedish design was in high demand at that time on the other side of the Atlantic. But it was also hard work. In Europe, Greta had felt thwarted as a woman in the industry. After finishing her studies, she applied for a job in Stockholm as a furniture designer in a department store and was rejected on the flimsy excuse that "We have no facilities for women." That's enough to transform a civilized woman into a praying mantis who bites the heads off the men who make such idiotic decisions—at least in her fantasies.

But if we want to find the inspiration behind the Gräshoppa, let's not confuse a homicidal mantis with a common grasshopper. Instead, let's think of the Gräshoppa as merry Flip from the *Maya the Bee* cartoon series. Greta probably saw a cheerful little chap just like him hopping around in a field while she was on her lunch break and he inspired the brilliant idea for the design of her next "it" piece for Hollywood's rich and beautiful. In any case, this animal catalyst engendered a magnificent lamp that's remarkable for its simplicity: three legs and a shade. Gräshoppa was perfectly in line with the minimalist mid-century modern movement and, in fact, has been in line with every stylistic era since—the mark of a true classic. The Danish design studio Gubi is now in charge of Greta's entire menagerie—the Swede had previously captured the spotlight with her Cobra wall lamp—and the question of women's rights has long been resolved. As Grossman herself once said, "The traditional idea that women aren't good at mechanical work is idiotic and absurd. The only advantage a male furniture designer might have is his physical strength." But actions speak louder than words. With her groundbreaking successes and prize-winning creations alone, Grossman has given the warehouse that once spurned her a one-finger salute.

The purist design of the floor lamp is reminiscent of a graceful grasshopper.

05

Swedish designer Greta Grossman worked in sunny California.

Below: A classic on every desk—the little sister of the famous Gräshoppa floor lamp.

20 Armchair

06

FAILURE OR NOT?
A true heavyweight that also used to carry around a nasty childhood disease.

Sculpture or seating furniture? The lady in the upper picture seems to be asking herself the same question.

Willy Guhl | 1954

Loop Chair

Perhaps it was sheer curiosity or the cheerful exuberance you sometimes experience when you bump into an old friend again after a long time. In any case, product designer Willy Guhl decided to pay his former student from the Kunstgewerbeschule a visit and stopped by his office at Eternit, a company in Niederurnen, Switzerland. Before long, Guhl and Robert Haussmann were having lunch at a nearby restaurant and letting their imaginations run wild. Eternit fiber cement was certainly not considered particularly sexy in the design scene, but Guhl was into experimenting with materials. As a neo-functionalist, he wanted to promote practical, low-cost housing, while as a designer he wanted to create flat-packed, mass-produced furniture suitable for the masses—Ikea would have been delighted with him. Until that point, Guhl had rarely encountered fiber cement. It's not surprising, since until then the panels had been mainly used in concrete roofing. Between soup and the main course (at least that's how I like to imagine it), the teacher and former student began wondering whether it might be possible to shape Eternit into curves and thus bid farewell to the austerity of straight lines. They decided to try hanging the panel over the edge of a table like a tablecloth before curing. The result was a planter known as the Biasca elephant's ear.

A nice try—and soon it actually became a successful product. This small victory spurred Guhl on. He eventually shaped and molded the material into a kind of endless loop that he intended to function as a beach chair. Although it was heavy, it looked light, and those who tried it out—guests at a public swimming pool—thought it was quite comfortable to sit on the concrete chair. Launched in 1954, it was celebrated, among other things, as the Loop Chair and exhibited in various museums. Until a problem was discovered in 1980: It contained asbestos for reinforcement. It had only been on display at the Museum of Modern Art in New York for two weeks before it was pulled from the museum due to health concerns. In response, German and Swiss employees applied a surface sealant to the chair—that would have to be enough. They had clearly followed Guhl's motto in life: Achieve the maximum with a minimum of effort.

In 1998, the chair's creator made improvements—the fiber cement was reformulated to work well without the asbestos. And because it was so attractive, the Loop Chair was also given a small table for the first time. With these heavyweights, you don't have to worry about them being stolen from your garden. Nor do you have to worry about gusts of wind blowing them away.

In the beginning, this was a material experiment: The heavyweight armchair consists of a fiber cement board connected to form an endless loop.

Walter Gropius | 1969

Tac 01

In the 1980s, the late TV host Joachim "Blacky" Fuchsberger once hosted an entire show in a nightshirt. Heartthrob Enrique Iglesias sped naked across the Mediterranean Sea on water skis. And Richard Branson, the CEO of Virgin Atlantic, pushed a beverage cart through the aisle of an airplane owned by his competitor, Air Aisa, dressed in a stewardess uniform. None of these celebrities made fools of themselves voluntarily. They had each lost a bet. It's always best to avoid such gambles unless you can be one hundred percent certain to win and never have to cash in your chips. Bauhaus founder Walter Gropius was well aware of this in 1967, when his friend, Philip Rosenthal, opened a porcelain factory in the picturesque town of Selb, Germany. Gropius refused to leave his adopted home in the United States, where he'd been living since the 1930s, to attend the opening. After all, he had designed the new building himself. He had visited it earlier, on which occasion Rosenthal led him on a tour of the premises. He checked out the canteen, admired the pool table, and gawked at the flamingos that strutted about the property. Rosenthal had acquired the birds to broaden the horizons of his employees. The two friends finally entered the production hall, where stacks of porcelain plates were waiting to be fired. They all seemed to be decked out in mourning, bearing black bands on their edges, and Rosenthal hastened to explain that the black color would turn to gold in the kiln. Gropius didn't believe a word of it. Perhaps he was thinking of all the times generations of alchemists had unsuccessfully tried to turn base metal into gold. And so he bet against his friend's claim. It was a gutsy move on his part. After all, Rosenthal knew better. The architect lost the wager, and to repay the debt, he agreed to design a pen for Rosenthal's pet pig, RoRo.

Typical Gropius: clear lines, sleek design and dominant edges.

In the end, however, Gropius's whirlwind visit to Selb not only resulted in additional architectural work, he also went home with a new idea. In the production hall, he had discovered some designs by his Finnish colleague, Tapio Wirkkala, for a set of dishes and thought to himself: "I can do that!" In 1969, he came up with his famous teapot, known as Service Tac 01. It had a streamlined aesthetic, based largely on triangles and semicircles, with a graceful shape and an ingenious lid with its own handle that solved an all too common problem. When pouring tea, most people take the precaution of resting one finger on the lid so that it won't fall off. The teapot for the Rosenthal Studio-Line was Gropius' final nod to posterity, for he died a short time later.

Unfortunately, the porcelain master's pet pig never moved into its new pen, even though Gropius had designed a truly luxurious domicile in the best Bauhaus style for dear old RoRo, complete with a stylish round entryway. The factory employees were against the idea. Perhaps they had reached their limit with the flock of pink birds wandering the premises. Nevertheless, RoRo did receive a different honor after his passing, when he was immortalized in a series of porcelain pigs in black, white, and pink. And his creator was none other than the designer Sebastian Herkner.

A triangle and a hemisphere were the inspiration for the Tac 01 service, whose most famous piece is the teapot.

Athos, Porthos, and Aramis really knew what friendship means: "All for one—and one for all," was the motto of the Three Musketeers. Heinz Rühmann acknowledged this special lifelong bond in 1930 when, in a trio with Willy Fritsch and Oskar Karlweis, he sang the words: "A friend, a good friend, is the best thing in the world." Most especially in uncertain times. But few things are more satisfying than a good pal who is always stands by you in all of life's moments. A support, something to hold onto, a person who is simply there whenever you need a friend.

And if a human pal is not around to get the job done, you may be forced to glance about your immediate surroundings and redefine your criteria. At some point, your gaze is certain to fall on something that is probably standing in an out-of-the-way corner in any home, just waiting to be called into service: a footstool. A simple implement that never says a word but is always ready to lend a hand without complaint. It may not be a friend, exactly, but it is a buddy.

And thus the Tolix footstool, designed in 1937 by the Frenchman Xavier Pauchard in Burgundy, also became a faithful companion. Hard as steel, battle-tried, incredibly resilient, it also makes things incredibly easy for its user. Although its steel frame was only one millimeter thick, it was folded and pressed so often in an elaborate manual process that it remained sturdy no matter where it stood. A hole in the seat made sure that water flowed off if it got caught in a rainstorm. The angled legs allowed the footstool to be stacked, and its rubber feet gave it stability on uneven ground. It had been through a lot, seen everything, offered assistance all around, and yet none of this seemed to have gone to its head. The footstool simply never tried to be something it was not. This fact was even expressed in Pauchard's original name for the stool: Tabouret H—

Xavier Pauchard | 1934

Tolix Stool

Footstool H. Plain and simple. Whether used as a seat, a support, a tabletop, or a short ladder, it was always near at hand and seemed to offer reassurance: Life may not be a box of chocolates, but together we are strong.

The early Tolix versions were footstools and chairs for offices, factories, and hospitals. Then it turned up at the World Fair in Paris before moving into countless numbers of family homes. The company remained family-owned, but faltered for a time in 2004. The owners considered giving up the business until Chantal Andriot, who worked in the accounting department, took over the company. In 2006, it was pronounced a Living Heritage Company, which is something like a nature conservancy, and one of the footstools can be seen at the Centre Pompidou. The Tolix now comes in many different styles, including 51 colors. Unfortunately, a great many cheap copies also exist. However, the original has managed to resist the ravages of time. After all, it can really take a beating. It's a friend for life. One for all, in fact.

09

Crystal balls represent beacons of hope. Evidently there are people who truly believe that they can look into them and see the future—preferably when the moon is full, because moonshine sheds more light on the subject. Of course, it's no good without an expert to interpret it—fortunetellers have to make a living, too. There are documented experiences that illustrate the brilliant properties of a glass ball: In the 13th century, people began to employ thick, transparent reading stones made of quartz when their eyesight weakened. In this sense, a crystal ball could be said to give a person second sight.

Tom Dixon | 2015

Melt

But some truly fascinating things can happen inside thick glass that make you lose sight of everything else. In 1963, British inventor Edward Craven-Walker looked deeply into the glass of an egg timer in a pub in Dorset. Walker was an entrepreneur and interested in natural states—he made nude underwater films, ran a nudist colony and—inspired by the sand running through the egg timer—began that very evening to experiment with orange juice bottles filled with different liquids. Somewhere along the way, he invented the first lava lamp in a decade that valued all manner of psychedelic experiences. The lamp made it onto TV series like *Dr. Who* and onto the list of products "Made in Britain" that make the United Kingdom so proud.

The shape of the mirrored lamp is reminiscent of a soap bubble that could burst at any moment.

With its iridescent surface, the Melt lamp by English designer Tom Dixon falls somewhere in between a crystal ball and a lava lamp. Wherever it hangs, people are drawn to take a closer look and penetrate its secrets. This work by the successful autodidact was supposedly a product of chance, created while he was playing around with materials—one of his favorite pastimes. When he first started designing with clay, he described the exhilarating feeling of molding a soft, amorphic blob into a beautiful object. "For me, that's the epitome of the transformation that makes design possible." As a former band musician—Dixon played bass guitar—he was well acquainted with metamorphoses: a handful of notes becoming an unforgettable melody and different instruments interacting to produce a complete work of art.

But let's stick with clay, which assumes a shape, melting glass that becomes an object, and the ugly duckling who's soon spreading its wings as a swan. Melt is a sphere that looks like an unfinished, melted lump of glass from a glassblower's workshop, a diamond in the rough. Melt could also pass as an asteroid from outer space, a piece that's out of this world—which is exactly what makes it an excellent design.

The Melt lamp is made with an exciting mix of materials, including polycarbonate with a copper, chrome or gold coating.

This Swiss tubular steel furniture impresses with the simplicity of its form, with lightness and functionality.

10

Battista und Gino Giudici | 1936

Lido

If things go well, vacations are spent in completely different spheres, in never-never land, on cloud nine, or in some similarly exclusive place of pure happiness. You should still try to restrain yourself a bit, because the danger is also high that you'll return to everyday life with some unnecessary ballast. By this I don't mean the superfluous pounds that you might put on at the hotel buffet or the pool bar, but the things that you are prepared to buy when you're overcome by that feeling you get when you see something truly beautiful. Delightful spices in a souk fog your senses, the mountain sun heats your brain, and before you know it, you suddenly find yourself with an engraved brass lamp in your hand, a reindeer skin under your arm, or small ornate stone jars in your pocket. At home, alas, you realize that such things don't fit in with the Mid-century modern ambience of your own apartment. And a word of warning about reindeer skins—it never takes long until they start to shed like crazy, believe me. Vacation souvenirs, even without annoying features, usually remain foreign elements in the comfortable surroundings you've settled into.

Unless, of course, you happened to be in Locarno at the lido beach resort on Lake Maggiore and decided to extend your vacation at home in the lounge chair that the locksmith Battista Giudici and his brother Gino designed in 1936 precisely for this establishment. The Lido lounger is a living piece of Ticino and comes without any folksy trappings. It looks like summer itself, buoyant, light, and bright red like poppies in the fields. It has long since evolved into a design icon, made it into the Schweizer Typenmöbel catalog, and was just given a few new colors for its 85th birthday: blue, yellow, and gray beige. Over the years, it has retained its most distinguished feature: It's a wonderful spot for dreaming. Of places that don't have to be far away. Just far enough away from everyday life.

Jaime Hayon | 2010

Monkey

In the 1960s, Frenchman Pierre Brassau stood out as an exceptionally talented artist. "Brassau paints with powerful strokes, but also with clear determination," enthused the Swedish columnist Rolf Anderberg in the Göteborgs-Posten. "His brush strokes twist with furious fastidiousness. Pierre is an artist who performs with the delicacy of a ballet dancer." What poor Anderberg didn't yet realize was that Pierre Brassau didn't exist. He was the invention of Journalist Ake Axelsson. And the paintings in Göteburg's Galerie Christianae that had garnered such extravagant praise from so many critics were the works of a chimpanzee named Peter. Axelsson asked zookeepers to put brushes, paint, and canvas in Peter's cage and give the chimpanzee a free hand, so to speak. He then transported the four most promising paintings to the gallery for what was a great joke for Axelsson and a grand humiliation for the art world. Is it only coincidental that we refer to mischievous shenanigans as "monkey business"?

In art, the ape is a serious motif in itself, although the monkey is usually the subject rather than the creator. In the 16th century, Singerie—French for "monkey trick"—was its own genre in which painters portrayed animals taking on the roles of humans. Johann Joachim Kaendler created a bestseller of its day in 1747 with his monkey orchestra made of Meissen porcelain. In 2006, artist Jörg Immendorff installed his famous Monkey Gate in front of the Salzburg Festspielhaus and Banksy, with his "Devolved Parliament" painting, parodied the British House of Commons by portraying it as a herd of monkeys. This animal that's so absurdly similar to us has also appeared now and then in the world of design. In Kay Bojesen's case, monkeys weren't really the point. Although he carved what are certainly the world's most famous designer monkeys, he also did more that that, leaving us with a complete bestiary made up of cute wooden creatures. But moving further along the timeline, we come straight to the exceptional Spanish talent Jaime Hayon, a prankster who, as a child, painted Snoopy characters on his mother's leather couch—which she did not appreciate—and once he became a successful artist, liked to hold interviews in a rabbit suit. It seems that Hayon is infatuated with our animal relatives. He has designed decorative monkey masks to hang on the wall and crowned a carousel—which he covered with 15 million tiny crystals and set before a mountain backdrop for the Swarovski Kristallwelten—with a human-sized chimpanzee. And then, of course, there's his legendary monkey side table that he conceptualized for BD Barcelona Design, "an unthinkable piece for any minimalist or rationalized catalog" according to its label, and presented as a complement to his garden furniture collection in 2015. As for Hayon himself, "I want to create something unique," he has said. "I want people to feel something when they encounter my pieces." Like an irresistible urge to stretch the corners of their mouths toward their ears? What's also known as smiling.

11

Maija Isola | 1964
Unikko

Not everyone can bear honest words, and some things are indeed better left unspoken. It is interesting, however, that entire societies sometimes agreed on things that it was better not to get too close to, even verbally: In the Middle Ages, the plague was vaguely called "the curse", and the Romans generally avoided the word "death" and preferred to speak of "weakness." Such linguistic restrictions are so-called taboo words, and usually there is superstition behind them. Even Harry Potter's classmates at Hogwarts would rather have bitten off their tongues than utter the name Voldemort. The somewhat awkward substitute for the Dark Lord: "He-Who-Must-Not-Be-Named." The Finns probably have little to do with wand-wielding villains, but their fear of evoking horror by calling it by its name is quite similar: They avoid speaking of bears because if they did, they are convinced, they would surely run into one. Indeed, such an encounter in the Nordic wilderness does not sound tempting. The Finnish substitute is "honey paw" or "forest apple". Sounds almost affectionate, doesn't it?

The taboo as a guarantee that you definitely won't get what you don't want? For Armi Ratia, head of the Finnish interior label Marimekko, this went thoroughly wrong: In 1964, she forbade her designers to create floral patterns because they would never achieve the beauty of a real flower. That was a clear message. Just as clear as designer Maija Isola's response: eight floral designs. Maija was apparently not so fond of orders, perhaps she was convinced that she could easily compete with nature. Armi Ratia could have responded with the typically Finnish words "haista kukkanen!" literally meaning "smell the flower," figuratively meaning "nuts to you!" Presumably, however, she simply had a coffee, which Finns are known to do all the time, and took a rather conciliatory look at the samples that lay before her. In the end, she gave her blessing to all eight floral designs of the rebellious Maija. Among them was Unikko, which means "poppy". And this one became Marimekko's bestseller and trademark. The cheerful pattern now decorates not only dishes and pillows, but also shower curtains, credit cards, bags and Manolo Blahnik shoes. "Loppu hyvin, kaikki hyvin"—all's well that ends well. Isn't Finnish wonderful?

Happy, colorful, Marimekko. A design icon that spreads good cheer—although the poppy pattern was not favored by Armi Ratia in the beginning.

13

Hans J. Wegner | 1949

Wishbone Chair

Obsessions are a thing. Some are brought to the brink of madness, others are driven to flights of fancy by them. The painter Salvador Dalí was so fascinated by the dream interpretation of the psychotherapist Sigmund Freud that he repeatedly used his symbolism in his paintings and traveled to Vienna several times on the off chance of meeting his great idol. The Japanese artist Yayoi Kusama, in turn, constantly creates new dream worlds full of dots. In the best case, a fixation gives creative power a clear direction, and from that point of view, designer Hans J. Wegner really couldn't complain: He had a thing for chairs; he was determined to design the one true, universally good seating. He designed his first chair at the tender age of 15. Over the course of his life, he would go on to design more than 500 different models of chairs, all made of wood in good Scandinavian tradition and in very organic shapes. The press was right to nickname him "Master of the Chair". Not every attempt turned out to be a great success, but his curriculum vitae was crowned by a number of icons: the Shell Chair, for example, or the Smiling Chair. In 1949, for example, the PP501, the Round Chair, made its career, and was soon known only as "The Chair". To be honest, this was not only due to its elegance, but also because John F. Kennedy and Richard Nixon held their legendary televised presidential debate on it. A short time later, the American magazine Interiors named it the most beautiful chair in the world. While the world was still celebrating The Chair, Wegner was already coming up with a follow-up piece, the Wishbone Chair. The master had based its seat shape on the style of the Chinese Ming Dynasty, and since the wooden struts in the backrest formed the penultimate letter in the alphabet, the Wishbone also became known as the Y-Chair and, due to its production at the Danish company Carl Hansen & Søn, numbered as the CH26. Of all things, the chair that brought him world fame did not make the master happy at all: He found the wooden Y in the back rather disturbing, the chair remained in his eyes not thought through to the end—clearly unfinished. For him, a single model would have sufficed as a complete work anyway: "If only one could make one good chair in a lifetime," he had once sighed. Only to note in the same breath, "but you just can't."

And speaking of obsessions, one nation has a particular passion for the Wishbone: the Japanese. More than a quarter of the chairs produced each year go directly to the Land of Smiles. There is even a book there that deals exclusively with this object of desire. This actually needs an update every year: just in time for the designer's birthday in April, Carl Hansen & Søn always brings a special limited edition of the bestseller onto the market. Sometimes in antique oak, sometimes in mahogany or with a leather seat. Let's see what they come up with next time.

The production of the Wishbone Chair requires more than 100 different steps, many of which are still carried out by hand today.

De Pas, D'Urbino and Lomazzi | 1973

Sciangai

The good old game of Mikado has gone somewhat out of style. When game aficionados want to show a steady hand, they are more likely to do so with a car-racing video game that while sitting at a table with a pile of colorful sticks. However, there is one place where Mikado is still ever-present: When German politicians accuse their opponents of inaction. Ever since the phrase "Beamten-Mikado" was first heard on the stage of a GDR cabaret, accompanied by the tongue-in-cheek explanation—"move first and you lose"—the game has been a metaphor for government inaction. The name itself originated in Japan, where the emperor was historically called the Mikado. Paradoxically, the game doesn't actually have anything to do with Asia. It was, in fact, invented in Europe. Did the Japanese name come about in Germany only because the sticks are reminiscent of chopsticks and are therefore associated with food culture in the land of the rising sun? Nowhere else did anyone make this connection. The game is called Spellicans in the UK, Jonchets in France, Spillikins in Canada, and Sciangai in Italy. Although the latter sounds a bit like Shanghai, it doesn't actually have anything to do with the Chinese city. It's all about the sticks—either being dropped while playing a game or serving as an object over which other things are dropped. Sciangai is namely a truly ingenious coat rack designed by the Italian trio of Jonathan De Pas, Donato D'Urbino, and Paolo Lomazzi for the furniture manufacturer Zanotta. The rack consists of eight long poles which are specially constructed to be folded up like a bundle of twigs with only one hand and to stand quietly in a corner when not in use. When opened vertically, the rods automatically fan out just like a game of Mikado, all ready to receive bags, coats, and jackets. The three founders of the DDL design studio once again demonstrated their wicked sense of humor when they came up with this oversized game in 1973. Their previous designs had included Blow (▶ p. 218), an enormous inflatable armchair from 1967, and Joe, a sofa from 1970, which looks like a huge baseball glove. They named the entire series "Radical Design." After all, even revolutions need to have a name, and usually also a kind of manifesto. "We were young in those days, with a zest for life, and we wanted to challenge bourgeois traditions," Lomazzi said years later.

Above all, they contributed a good bit of fun to the industry. A certain playfulness, you could say. And we can never get too much of that.

The smart clothing rack folds easily for storage.

Sebastian Herkner | 2014

Oda

If you want to open a business or launch a successful new product on the market, common business wisdom suggests that you find a niche. Offer something surprising and unexpected, something that creates a need that most people never even knew they had. Find something that no one else was even looking for. Looked at in this way, the photographer duo Bernd and Hilla Becher did everything right. Instead of supplying the world with images of the same old motifs, they specialized in framework houses and industrial buildings, factories, gasometers, grain silos and, in 1957, water towers in Europe and the U.S. As of 1976, they both taught photography at Kunstakademie Düsseldorf, where Bernd Becher became the first-ever professor. One of their most famous students was photographic artist Andreas Gursky. It doesn't take shared genes for one generation to pass expertise and passion down to another. You might say that the Bechers were indirectly responsible for a host of beautiful photos and, by extension, for an image of a lamp: the Oda. Its German designer, Sebastian Herkner, saw the Becher's photos of water towers, drove from Frankfurt to Munich to see them in person, and had an epiphany. He would place a balloon full of light on top of an elegant metal structure. Herkner, who at that time was the brightest new star in the interior design firmament when it came to inspiration, was also a practical man and well-grounded. He entrusted Patrizia Moroso, the label queen, with his idea for the anti-slip Coat sofa, which at that time took the form of non-slip children's socks with rubber grips.

All of his ideas are everyday life-friendly and down-to-earthness seems to run in his family. It wasn't until Herkner designed an entire house of the future at imm Cologne—a true badge of honor for the newcomer—that his mother finally realized that her son was famous, although during the fair, she was inside the house washing the glasses. Refreshingly normal.

Originally from Offenbach, Germany, Herkner not only worked for top fashion designer Stella McCartney, but also did internships in all sorts of handicrafts. Because he had been fascinated by colorful church windows as a child, he was especially fond of looking over the shoulders of glassblowers and he really pushed them to their limit for the XL Oda. A glass globe of that size is the result of a lot of trial and error as well extremely hard work.

Although Herkner's workaholism is legendary, he still finds time to watch TV. He once saw his Oda on the Sunday evening crime series *Tatort*. His reaction: "At least it wasn't in the murderer's living room."

In 2008, the design bible *Wallpaper* named the cheeky little monkey the epitome of Danish design.

46   Toy

16

Kay Bojesen | 1951

Monkey

The Danes are known for their love of cuddly things, and apparently they have also developed a soft spot for furry critters: Every ninth citizen of our neighboring country owns a dog, and the Danish royal family has a number of dachshunds. Despite their love of animals, unfortunately the Danes still have a law on the books that dates back to 1872, according to which landowners are entitled to shoot any dogs and cats that venture onto their property. One animal enjoys closed season, however, and is free to venture anywhere. In fact, it can be found in nearly half of all households—Kay Bojesen's wooden monkey. It's a popular gift for babies, and at some point it moves from the children's room to the living room, where it proudly sits on the bookshelf or desk. For the rest of its life.

The fact that Bojesen, a Danish silversmith, came up with the monkey was probably due to a well-known phenomenon: When men become fathers, they undergo a noticeable change. They gain an average of four kilos during their wives' pregnancies, and one in five men simultaneously suffers from nausea and back pain. And thus wild guys sometimes mutate into tame husbands. We know from Paul Maar, creator of the fictional *Sams* character, that he started writing children's books from one moment to the next. Something also happened to Bojesen when his son Otto was born in 1919. He found himself suddenly dragging teak and limba wood into his workshop, and then began using his lathe to create funny wooden animals that would delight more than just little Otto. At some point, this mini zoo went into mass production and became truly famous. But it was the monkey that really stole the show. Although his creation only dates to 1951, long after Otto had outgrown the nursery, the little animal achieved cult status as a design piece. Monkey business? Not at all! With its playful spirit, principle of "form follows function" (after all, long arms have certainly proven their worth in terms of evolution), and the silky smoothness of the wood, this primate quite simply demonstrates real style. In the meantime, the Rosendahl Design Group has even reissued a few forgotten creatures from the Bojesen collection. Childish? Absolutely—and that's what's so wonderful about it. Norwegian playwright Henrik Ibsen once said: "In this beautiful world, there is nothing more clever you can do than to play." It's no wonder that Scandinavians are among the happiest people in the world.

The wooden monkey with character has become a coveted collector's item.

Dieter Rams and Dietrich Lubs | 1987

AB 1 Alarm Clock

Just as city dwellers can't stop raving about the peaceful life in the countryside—which gets on the nerves of old-established farm dwellers—more than a few contemporaries like to indulge in the erroneous assumption that generations up to the last century did not know any hustle and bustle. And anyway: everything was better in the past. Granted, the word deadline probably didn't exist, but of course our ancestors didn't wander around timelessly. The fact that the first alarm clocks were invented at an astonishingly early date in ancient times, suggests that people back then also had good reasons to get things done on time and to hurry with their tasks. Because the mechanics of the timers were still missing at that time, a float in a water-filled vessel triggered a little bell at a certain water level—that was the signal that it was now high time. For whatever. In medieval monasteries, people already relied on alarm clocks to keep time for prayers, and at the turn of the modern age, the first travel alarm clock was invented in the form of the officer's alarm clock: The men often slept outside the barracks and wanted to be on time for morning roll call. Finally, industrialization forced whole armies of workers and employees to wake up early; in fact, at that time, Black Forest clocks initially took care of the wake-up call.

In the 1960s, the mechanics and technology in all clocks and watches flirted ever more fiercely with design, and so the Braun company (yes, the one with the razors) also afforded itself a team of designers, who taught the humble pocket calculators, useful clockwork and the like of it good, but simple and functional manners. The young interior designer Dieter Rams, who had been with the company since 1955, was particularly eager and passionate about his work. His nickname: Mr. Braun, his job: to design Braun appliances in such a way that they were compatible with the modern interiors of the time. Rams was into Bauhaus design, and his design was based on ten theses of his own making, which he didn't have to bang on a door to hammer into his employees: For him, the perfect form was above all logical, simple, honest and beautiful. One of his most ardent fans may have been his employee Dietrich Lubs, a young shipbuilder who had joined the Rams team in 1962 from the Hansa shipyard in Cologne. Together, Lubs and Rams designed watches and calculators—and the ingeniously simple and thus simply beautiful AB 1 alarm clock from the 1980s. Black and white dial, two hands for clock and alarm time, a yellow second hand, packed into a compact, pleasing, slightly rounded case. Simple, but poignant. True to the spirit of its inventors. In terms of design of everyday things, a real awakening.

There is a wonderful love story surrounding Ingo Maurer. The designer was still fairly unknown, had indulged in an entire bottle of wine in Venice, and returned slightly ticked off to his inexpensive boarding house, where he stared at the naked light bulb above his bed. We don't know what he discovered there, but the result must have been an epiphany of sorts, a moment when he fell for its bare, naked light. His aspirations as a designer changed direction after that: he detested lampshades ever since, he wanted to "actually see light and have a tender relationship with it".

His first design, Bulb, in 1967 was little more than a light bulb; further development followed in 1992, when he equipped it with airy little wings made of white goose feathers and two wires that led into its innermost part like arteries to a burning heart. Finally, "Porca Miseria!" was followed by a luminous structure not unlike a pile of shards hung under the ceiling, and in 1997, finally, Zettel'z. The thing looked as if one had blown up an overflowing desk tray with forms, papers, documents of all kinds. For this purpose, Maurer draped DIN A 5 Japanese papers on wires around a light source that now looks at best like an incandescent lamp, but has of course long since been an LED variant.

Ingo Maurer | 1997

Zettel'z

40 of the papers were printed, and 40 without words and without content—an invitation to the creativity of the owners. You could paint them, write curses or aphorisms on them, or even plain appointment reminders. The invitation to creative development was, by the way, put to good use: Blushing Zettel'z, for example, was equipped with little papers on which Chinese porcelain figures contorted themselves in all kinds of erotic poses. Maurer had once again outdone himself: with wit, genius, and the imagination to simply think things differently. And he had staged light once again without having to create a lampshade. So he remained true to himself: "Design where you no longer feel the person behind it bores me," he had once said. Maurer died in 2019 at the age of 87. A shining light, of course. Zettel'z remains—a dream.

A beautiful Zettel'z takes time and creativity for adjusting the sticks and selecting and designing the leaves.

18

Erik Magnussen: He set the bar for the tea pot design.

54 Vacuum jug

19

Eric Magnussen | 1977

Stelton EM77

Footsteps are always too big, somehow. Especially the ones we leave on the earth's ecosystem. But the ones that people step into as they follow their role models or predecessors are just as large. Mick Schumacher, the racecar driver's son, will always have to measure his success against that of his speedy father. When Virginie Viard, assistant to Chanel designer Karl Lagerfeld, launched her first collection for the Parisian luxury label after the fashion czar's death, the entire industry criticized her handling of founder Coco Chanel's treasured legacy. But then *Le Figaro* offered her absolution with the words: "The spirit of Mademoiselle lives on, as does the spirit of Karl Lagerfeld." Viard didn't mess up. Good for her.

Rising-star designer Erik Magnussen also came under intense scrutiny in 1976 when the Danish home accessory label Stelten asked him to design a few nice pieces for the company. He was to replace architectural heavyweight Arne Jacobsen, who had passed away several years earlier. Magnussen faced two outcomes: either win the biggest stakes of his life or fail miserably. Did he pass sleepless nights? Tear out his hair in despair? Maybe. Whatever the case, he would have felt the intense loneliness that comes from the wordless accusation of a pristine, blank sheet of paper. That "do something!" The brutal imperative that drives authors to struggle with writer's block in similar situations. Without a doubt, this pressure lent him wings in the end. In any case, he presented Stelton Manager Peter Holmblad, who just happened to be Jacobsen's stepson, the idea

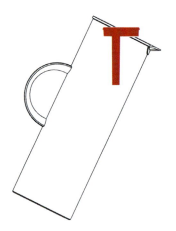

for a vacuum jug the following year. Its cylindrical shape was reminiscent of the famous Cylinda-line tableware designed by the Danish master, although its rounded handle also had softer lines. Magnussen and Holmblad went on to refine the thermos's revolutionary rocker stopper.

The vacuum jug was launched under the name EM77. It soon became a worldwide success in stainless steel and plastic, clothed time and again in new seasonal colors. It won the Klassikerprisen, the coveted Danish design prize, the only piece to ever do so twice.

What lessons can we derive from this? The fact that you must either grow past your own capabilities and into the footsteps of those who've gone before. Or you must take an entirely new path, away from the giant steps of your role model. In this sense, Magnussen played a strong hand. Indeed, if you place a bet, you will win. Some of the time, at least.

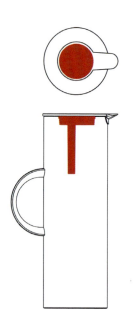

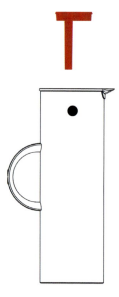

Ingenious function, timeless design: The Stelton teapot still enjoys great popularity today.

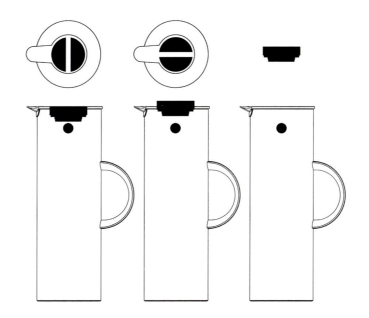

„Mr. X" | 1950s

Acapulco Chair

According to a recent Harvard study, sunbathing acts a bit like opiates—endorphins are apparently released into the skin. But anyone who has ever dozed off at the beach or beside a pool also knows that too much sunshine can make you feel sluggish. To say nothing of the damage to your skin.

In 1953, however, an unknown French tourist had a completely different problem during his vacation in Acapulco: When he sat down on a poolside chair, he suffered a nasty burn to his rear end because the seat was so hot. He seems to have kept a rather cool head otherwise, however, because he immediately started mulling over a solution to the problem. He ended up inventing something of a hybrid between the hammock common among the indigenous Mayans and a modern armchair. Plastic cords instead of a continuous seat made it more airy, and before long it became the absolute "it" piece—even though back during the mid-century there probably would have been another way of expressing it.

This attractive blend of Mexican tradition and chic lifestyle became known as the Acapulco chair. The fact that America's rich and famous had been vacationing mainly on the Pacific coast of Mexico around Acapulco since the Cuban Revolution made it just as famous as all of the Celebrities who relaxed in it, including Elizabeth Taylor, Frank Sinatra, the Kennedys, John Wayne, and Elvis Presley. In other words, all the usual suspects.

The chair's creator has remained the great unknown, Mr. X, so to speak. This is unusual in an industry that puts so much stock in names that it often turns into a vanity fair. The fact that the Acapulco chair became so popular naturally attracted a lot of imitators—especially considering that there was no registered patent without an official inventor. Among the countless versions, there are unfortunately a lot of cheap imitations—some of which even use a covering fashioned out of simple clotheslines. And the original? A Danish company and a fair-trade manufacturer from Mexico offer themselves as answers. The only true version? Who knows? The Frenchman of yesteryear, having written such a sunny chapter in design history, has fallen silent, possibly forever. If he had been paid for his flash of inspiration, he would have earned a pretty penny. Far more than he would have received as compensation for his overheated backside.

20

Christian Dell | 1933

Kaiser Idell 6631

A fierce wind is currently blowing through the most popular hotels, restaurants, and cafés: Industrial style is one of the latest hypes, with lots of metal, bare concrete, glass, and wood. Unpolished, raw, often with corners and edges. A style that smacks of the calluses, sweat, and the hard work of tough guys. One that transforms the world of factories and factory halls into a lifestyle ambience. Strictly speaking and from a historical perspective, this is an aberration since the working atmosphere that industrialization introduced into society after World War I was anything but cozy. The machines never stood still, and people often labored late into the night under artificial lights. This was also the case at the Auma factory in the German state of Thuringia, where workers diligently made tools for the production of industrial porcelain.

One night in 1919, when engineer Curt Fischer was walking through the rows on the late shift, he noticed that the quality of the parts deteriorated as soon as the workers had to lean forward and work in their own shadows. Fischer hurried to his own, presumably better lit, workstation and devised a wall light that could be pulled from left to right thanks to an accordion arm. It was the first model of a scissor lamp, which from that point on also symbolized the shifting requirements for light.

Fischer's design served as inspiration for the Bauhaus, where master metalworker Christian Dell further refined the scissors principle in 1931 to create lamps that are now highly sought after by vintage fans. Later, however, he also searched for lighting designs that would be suitable for other work areas—after all, desk workers had a need for the odd bit of enlightenment as well. The exciting thing about these generations of lamps that were designed as workhorses is that they were chock-full of technology, even apart from all the electrical components—thanks to intelligent joints and springs, glare-free reflectors, and similar innovations. Dell's masterpiece for accountants and other office workers was the 6631 luxury table lamp with a patented swivel ball joint connection that made it possible for users to adjust and direct the light as needed. After his time at the Bauhaus, he designed it for Gebrüder Kaiser & Co. in Neheim in the Sauerland region.

Although the Gebrüder Kaiser & Co. lamp factory went bankrupt in 1980, Dell's table lamp is one of many Kaiser Idell models now manufactured in Denmark by Fritz Hansen. The name Kaiser Idell was a play on words inspired by combining Kaiser, Dell, and the German word for idea (Idee). Trained as a silversmith, at some point Christian Dell decided to return to his roots and opened a jewelry store in Wiesbaden. He died a wealthy man in 1975. If he ever happened to watch a crime series on TV in the evenings after work, he very likely saw an old acquaintance greeting him from the screen. Starting in the 1950s, the model he had invented as a perfect desk lamp became a star in the crime world. It appeared during countless interrogations in police offices in series ranging from *Der Kommissar* to *Tatort*, which earned the little beauty its nickname as the "commissioner's lamp." In many respects, it brought light into the darkness. An excellent piece of work.

The Bocca lip sofa is considered an icon of Italian Radical Design. In the USA, it is also known as the Marilyn Monroe Sofa, a tribute to the legendary Hollywood diva.

22

Studio 65 | 1970

Bocca

There are walk-in closets, walk-in attics, walk-in art installations—and, since Salvador Dalí, walk-in faces. For his own museum in Figueres, he created a room that from a gallery looks like a woman's face: The two pictures on the wall become eyes, the chimney-like sculpture between them becomes a nose, and the sofa in the shape of lips becomes—of course— the mouth. "Mae West's Face Which May Be Used as a Surrealist Apartment," was the title Dalí gave his painting from 1934. The optical illusion of a room that looks like a woman's head is modeled after Mae West, an extraordinarily sexy bombshell.

One thing is clear: Without this painting, the lip sofa would never have existed. Dalí's patron, the hardly less eccentric but far richer Edward James, was the one who first gave the artist the idea of turning his dreams into reality, so to speak. Five sofas were initially produced in England in 1936/37, turning a work of art into a product intended for everyday use. A genuine piece of pop art, long before the term was even

64 Sofa

invented. It stands to reason that Dalí had indeed been inspired by Mae West's lips for the piece, though he sometimes later claimed it was just a sculpture he had modeled after a pile of rocks near Cadaqués, where he liked to spend time with his wife Gala. His attempt to distance himself sounds a bit clumsy, especially since we know that he was obsessed with the actress. Mae West didn't give a damn about the usual conventions in prudish America; after all, the femme fatale had been sentenced to jail for her self-written play "Sex" in 1927, and she preached free love.

In real life, Mae West's lips had thinned somewhat by that time due to age, and so the relevance of Dalí's sofa was slightly diminished by the time Gufram, the interior design label known for its craziness, came up with a very similar sofa called Bocca in 1970. It had been created by the designers of the Studio 65 group headed by architect Franco Audrito as a rather purpose-built detail of a Milan fitness center—for a temple of beauty, as the men smugly remarked. They initially named the sofa "Marilyn" as a tribute to the *Some Like It Hot* actress who embodied the ideal of beauty—and because the owner of the gym happened to share the same name. But they hastened to concede that Dalí's original had, of course, been the inspiration.

The Bocca became a shooting star: It was on stage during tours by Beyoncé, Kylie Minogue, and Katy Perry, and famous photographers such as Richard Avedon and Rankin chose it as a prop that sometimes even upstaged the models themselves. It became a contemporary representative of pop art and the Italian radical design movement. Is it possible they envied the fame of the uninvited twin sister? Who knows. In 1973, at any rate, Dalí's two-seat lip sofa went into series production at BD Barcelona. Although Mae West's lips eventually ended up in museums around the world, Marilyn was adapted to the zeitgeist from time to time. Since 2008, the Bocca sofa has also been available in two additional versions: Dark Lady featuring a Gothic style in black and with a piercing, and Pink Lady, which would make Barbie happy as well.

Did they take the words out of her mouth? Let's just say they pay lip service, because you never really know where you stand.

Incidentally, the historical model for the
Pop Art Sofa was Salvador Dalí's Dalilips Sofa
from 1936.

Former Italian Prime Minister Silvio Berlusconi probably threw away his chances forever with the Finns: When the decision was made to base the European Food Safety Authority (EFSA) in Parma in 2005, beating out Helsinki as a potential site, Berlusconi quipped that Italy had been the better choice because Finnish food, especially smoked reindeer, tasted awful. In fact, the Finns could at best be considered as hosts of an EU authority for models. "I love Finnish women," he added. "The main thing is that they are of legal age." The insulted northerners took their revenge with a reindeer-covered flatbread they named the "Berlusconi pizza"—and with which they easily beat out the Italians at a pizza competition in New York.

It would be wrong to conclude that these two rivals, representing the top and bottom of Europe, cultivate fundamentally irreconcilable differences, as design history shows: In 1966, at any rate, both countries presented their best sides in something of a joint project—the Bolle vase series. Tapio Wirkkala, a solitary Finnish designer who lived so deep in the woods that prototypes of his designs had to be flown to him by helicopter, apparently decided to emerge from the wilderness one day and flew to Venice. At the Venini glassworks, he had the artisans show him a glassblowing technique known as incalmo that was developed during the Renaissance. The process involved working with two spheres of glass, cutting them, and then later fusing them together again. The method had fallen into obscurity, and not without good reason—there was simply too much breakage in the process. Wirkkala was so fascinated that he designed a collection of vases made of two different colors of glass and pestered the Italians until they were able to use the old technique to craft the gossamer glass bodies without breakage.

Tapio Wirkkala | 1966

Bolle

Yes, these vases made of exquisite Murano glass are enchantingly beautiful. And no, I wouldn't want any of them. Can you imagine putting flowers in one and setting it on a sideboard? Only behind bulletproof glass! After all, they cost as much as a small car—but unfortunately they don't come with a bumper.

The five-piece bottle series has been one of Venini's classics since it was designed in 1966.

23

Minimalism-fan Eero Aarnio simply removed all the corners—this is how the Ball Chair was created.

Armchair

Anyone who wants to learn how grand entrances work should take a look at some classics from movie history. Staircases regularly play important supporting roles, such as when, in *The Princess Diaries*, Julie Andrews descends a marble staircase in such an elegant manner that even her unsuspecting movie granddaughter Anne Hathaway realizes that her grandma really is a queen. Or the scene in *Titanic* in which Kate Winslet as Rose floats down the first-class staircase wearing a dream dress to meet her Jack, alias Leonardo DiCaprio, who is speechless with delight. Both scenes are about the viewer suddenly seeing the main character with different eyes, and experiencing a sudden realization: that the nice old lady does in fact rule a kingdom, or that it's all over for the protagonist. The staircase elevates this moment and makes it magical. A job that, in film history, is sometimes entrusted to armchairs as well. Do you remember *You Only Live Twice*, the James Bond movie from 1967? There's a scene in which an armchair, which we only see from behind, slowly turns towards the audience, revealing a view of the villain Blofeld, smiling complacently as he strokes a white cat. Why on earth did the director choose a rather boring leather chair instead of Eero Aarnio's ingenious Ball Chair? Incomprehensible.

Aarnio originally designed the chair in 1963, initially only for himself, his wife Pirkko, and their two daughters. He vowed to his wife, "I'm going to create an armchair that people can't just walk past when it's in the store window." To do this, he drew a circle on paper, cut off a slice of it, and drew a foot to go with it. Commercial success, however, was a long time coming. A furniture store in Lahti, Finland, declined with thanks, but Aarnio didn't give up. He painted the shell of the chair red, stuck an enlarged Coca-Cola logo on the back, and had Pirkko sit in it and pose with a bottle of Coke. He sent the photos to the beverage giant, but once again received a rejection. It was not until the 1966 Cologne furniture fair that the time was apparently ripe

Eero Aarnio | 1963

Ball Chair

for the futuristic sphere made of fiberglass. The soundproofed piece was hailed as a sensation. Aarnio had finally made good on the promise he had once made to his wife.

Don't you think you could make a grand entrance or two in the Ball Chair? It's certainly worth a try. Position yourself with your back to the entrance, wait for a member of your family to come through the door, and then very slowly turn around. Surprise! With or without a cat. The chair also works as a surprise egg.

Natural shapes and feminine curves
inspired these luminaires.

70   Ceiling light

25

Serge Mouille | 1951

Araignée

Some people are said to be enraptured by chance encounters with celebrities. Gérard Depardieu shopping in the same supermarket where you happen to be standing at the cheese counter during your visit to Paris, Hugh Grant two tables away in a café, or Angela Merkel coming toward you while you're out on a hike—cool stuff. Yet all these celebrities are, of course, just people who buy cheese for dinner, need a coffee break now and then, and enjoy hobbies. Or, if they have children, they might have to show up at a parent-teacher conference now and then, or maybe even organize a student exchange for their offspring. In the latter case, it is a well-known fact that student exchanges are like Russian roulette for both the host family and the arriving student, or—as Forrest Gump would say—it's a bit like a box of chocolates; you never know what you're going to get.

In any case, a boy from Mosbach named Martin Nerbel was very lucky when it came to the host family he was assigned in the 1970s. During an exchange trip, he and a friend from school ended up in Paris with the great designer Serge Mouille. A slightly eccentric lady picked up the two 16-year-olds from the train station and carted

them off to an old stone house that Nerbel initially thought was a barn—but which turned out to be chock full of design, art, and collectibles. "For the two of us boys from middle-class backgrounds, it was a completely different world," Nerbel recalls today. It was the world of a design superstar.

From then on, every day the adolescents would explore their host father's workshop, where he would show them the blanks of his famous lights and explain his drawings. They marveled at his collections of fossils and nature sketches, and it was only years later that Nerbel truly understood that he had stood before the sources of inspiration for some of the greatest designs of the century: Mouille's lights, such as snail, Saturn—and, of course, Araignée, the spider. It became the centerpiece of the master's Noir series, with which he wanted to "set the room in motion."

Although Mouille died in 1988, the friendship with the Nerbel family endured. The former exchange student, in fact, later became a lighting designer in charge of marketing the reissue of his former host father's light fixtures. The Spider has long been a design icon and is still being made in France today, more than three decades after the death of its creator, using the original tools from the 1950s. Because of space reasons alone, the seven-legged metal monster is most beautiful hovering on high ceilings of old buildings. The finely forged lamp shades, however, also turn the much smaller pieces in the series into real showstoppers. Incidentally, Mouille did not have the animal world in mind while designing these particular pieces, but rather drew inspiration from some very human attributes: That is why he called them "Tétine"—which simply means tits. At the time, however, Mouille did not reveal this to his two host sons from Germany.

The simple yet eye-catching luminaire beautifies the room even when switched off.

These days, everybody's talking about childhood trauma. Some people just can't forgive their parents. A cruel restriction of their candy intake or of their time in front of the TV was apparently enough to destroy the relationship. It's an insult to those who have experienced real family trauma and continue to suffer from it throughout their lives. It's hard to know how designer Finn Juhl would rate his own experiences, but I think he'd have had a lot to contribute to a self-help group. As a little boy, he always had to request an audience with his father if he wanted to speak to him, and until he was called in, he would dutifully wait by a chimneypiece with an ugly clock on the mantel and an equestrian statue beside it. During his long wait, Juhl had plenty of time to think about style—and about comfortable furniture to sit on.

Finn Juhl | 1941

Poeten

Maybe these circumstances were also responsible for his developing a distinctly oppositional character. He seemed to have decided not to put up with anything and not to play by other people's rules. He became a free spirit who had no interest in fashion or trends. For him, furniture was an art and art could do whatever it wanted. At his father's insistence, he gave up on his dream of studying art history and instead pursued architecture in Copenhagen. But in 1937, he abandoned the pure theory of ceiling and wall ratios and structural engineering in order to design his own furniture—self-taught and with no training in carpentry. In 1940, he designed the Pelican, a chair with a curvier shape than was usual for the time. One year later, he presented an upholstered two-seater at the Copenhagen Cabinetmaker's Guild exhibition that he'd actually intended to put in his own house. People were drawn not just to his elegant sofa, but also to its companion, a plaster sculpture by the artist Sigurjón Ólafsson. This design reaffirmed Juhl's outrageous statement, that furniture and art go hand in hand and are sometimes even one and the same thing. The industry must have interpreted his sofa as a raised middle finger. His upholstery hid the structural elements, which meant it was in exact opposition to the modernism that was so trendy at the time. And one more affront: Juhl's attractive two-seater was also so complex that it wasn't mass-producible—at a time when Scandinavians were striving to democratize design and create only simple and functional pieces.

So Juhl played the part of a revolutionary, but it didn't harm his career. With his breakthrough in the U.S., he became an international—and soon a prizewinning—star designer. He designed the interior of an entire SAS airplane and furnished the Danish embassy in Washington. He was more commercial than other designers but he never had anything against being accessible to all. The house that was built for him and his family in 1942 is now open to the public as part of the Ordrupgaard Art Museum. But don't confuse his historic home with the House of Finn Juhl, the Danish design studio that currently manufactures the Poet sofa. By the way, the sofa's name didn't come from its creator. In 1958, a Danish cartoonist drew the sofa as a place where young poets ponder their lives and it has been called the Poet ever since.

Heinrich Heine once said: "When God gets bored in Heaven, he simply opens his window and looks out over the boulevards of Paris." If he assumed that the Heavenly Father reserved a special place in his heart for French flair, he was certainly not alone. Ever since the French Revolution at the end of the 17th century, French style has been the highest expression of our appreciation for luxury goods. However, the Paris boulevards that Heine mentioned can be described in many ways other that entertaining. Many a tourist on a sightseeing trip will have noticed how extraordinarily long they are. Heine's contemporary Victor Hugo therefore found that Paris involves a whole lot of walking. He is absolutely right. The city center extends around eleven kilometers from east to west, nine kilometers north to south. This may seem like a compact area, but it can

The famous Luxembourg chair: harmonious lines, maximum comfort and stackable functionality.

76   Chair

Paris Parks Department | 1923

Luxembourg chair

be a real endurance test for the feet. It is therefore a big relief to have reached the beautiful jardin du Luxembourg, situated between Saint-Germain-des-Prés and the Latin Quarter, where you can sink into one of the steel chairs placed there. At that moment, you most likely don't give a damn that you are sitting on an icon, one that was created specifically for this by the Paris Parks Department in 1923, before going on to conquer half the world.

It was a time when Europeans were dancing the Charleston and Coco Chanel lounged about in her cloche hat on living room sofas arranged in front of ornate coffee tables. These were "les années folles," the Roaring Twenties. The Bauhaus style, with its objectivity, was still in its infancy when the city on the Seine took a broad view of architecture and placed these pure green chairs in the park in front of the Senate building. Even today, a century later, they still simply grab attention with a minimalism that is strangely modern. However, until 1974, you had to pay a fee for a much-needed rest and a comfortable seat, a practice that also applied to the lounge chairs farther south on Mediterranean beaches. Note to self: Not everything used to be better. And at one point, something had to be done about the material from which the classic model was made. The current manufacturer, Lyon-based Fermob, experimented with ways to make the seat more comfortable and switched from steel to aluminum, at least for the everyday version. They also added more color in 24 different shades. Paris is always worth a trip, but if you end up going somewhere else, you will also find the Luxembourg chair in Harvard Yard, at the Amsterdam Zoo, and on Schlossplatz in Stuttgart, Germany. The choice is yours. And it won't cost you a penny. Or simply place a pair of the fine beauties in your own garden. And dream of Paris.

78 Candleholder

28

Mogens Lassen | 1962

Kubus

You had a subject at school that you hated, of course. And I'm guessing it was mathematics. It's just a guess, but statistically speaking I'm way ahead of the game with my prediction. The few math fans out there are sure to disagree, and they usually list things that wouldn't work without number crunching: Airplanes wouldn't take off, houses wouldn't be able to withstand strong gusts of wind. For Fields Medal winner Cédric Villani, Cambridge professor Ian Stewart, and other greats in the discipline, math is simply sexy: the poetry of prime numbers, the pure aesthetics of the mysterious unknown X (which once annoyed us as schoolchildren), the beauty of mathematical laws. And they're probably even right. Because apart from airplanes, robots, refrigerators, and magnificent buildings, math can also be found at home in small everyday design objects. That's logical, because it's all about the design language, and there's no getting around triangles, squares, octahedrons, circles, spheres and, of course, the cube.

As we know, cubes have six equal sides, but in the design world the term has become inseparably linked with the four-armed candleholder designed by Danish architect Mogens Lassen, who had a real soft spot for numbers and shapes. For weeks he sat in his studio, precisely calculating the relationships between the individual sides and, on this basis, fine-tuning the precise proportions for his ingenious geometric masterpiece. Whenever he was in danger of suffocating in the jumble of numbers, he would send his beloved toy steam engine rattling around the drawing board. Its puffing would kick his mind into high gear, ultimately getting Lassen's genius back on track—and thus bringing the project to a successful conclusion without any detours.

Furrier and fashion guru Birger Christensen was so fascinated by the Kubus candleholder that he purchased the very first copy, hid it behind the drapes at a dinner party, and ceremoniously unveiled it in the evening in front of the astonished guests. Incidentally, the original version of the Kubus was intended to hold eight candles, but Lassen reduced the number to four. He simply shortened it uniformly on all sides. Pure mathematics, just like we learned in school. And so the circle is closed, this geometric beauty: Add a little here, take away a little there, until the equation adds up—and in the end, poetry and aesthetics triumph.

By the way, Mogen's grandson, Søren Lassen, continues to run the design company "by Lassen." He recently added a vase to the Kubus collection. With a half sphere in the middle. Design language really is a wonderful thing!

The Altorfer deck chair, popularly known as the „spaghetti chair," is one of the best-known Swiss design classics, along with the Lido Lounger.

80   Deck chair

Huldreich Altorfer jr. | 1948

Altorfer Deck Chair

Anyone who assumes that, as the child of an entrepreneur, all you have to do is settle down in your nice little nest is very much mistaken. After all, in Thomas Mann's novel *Buddenbrooks*, the first-born son of the company's founder was disinherited simply because he did not marry in a manner befitting his station. Examples of disastrous relationships between senior and junior can also be found in real life: In the Falk city map dynasty, for instance, son Alexander squandered his entire inheritance and ended up in prison at some point, while the three daughters of fashion emperor Steilmann all failed, one after the other, at the helm of their father's company.

Business experts estimate that half of all father-to-son or father-to-daughter successions go thoroughly wrong. And there are plenty of reasons for this: Farmers' sons, faced with the constant need to get up early, meet milk quotas, and other obstacles, sometimes decline with thanks when it comes to taking over the family farm—or perhaps the father ends up keeping a constant watchful eye on everything his exhausted progeny does, even at a ripe old age. Things rarely go as smoothly as in the clan of a German clothing company, whose eldest wrote the following prophetic words in an autograph book while he was still a boy: "I want to be the boss of Trigema when I grow up."

Sometimes, however, entrepreneurial offspring find their way to success precisely because they put a certain distance between themselves and the family business. Huldreich Altorfer Jr. had risen through the ranks from being a commercial assistant at Embru, an iron and metal bed factory commanded by his father in Switzerland, to become Vice Director. After his father's death, however, the company refused to let him take over as Director. So he quit in order to do his own thing. He founded Altorfer AG in Wald and Oberdürnten. Was this an act of liberation, even from a spiritual point of view? We will never know. In any event, three years later he introduced a revolutionary deck chair made of tubular steel and colorful plastic cord, which, after a minor modification, made it possible for users to rock in a wonderfully comfortable supine position. It became a big hit and was awarded a design prize in 1964. But sometimes karma strikes back; business, like Switzerland itself, has its ups and downs. The competition, insulted after Junior quit, did not sleep: In 1971, Embru took over his company—and the deck chair right along with it. Still, both then and now, things are going like clockwork for the deck chair, and it has miraculously remained the same despite the back and forth of company politics: The tubular frame is still manufactured in Rüti, not far from Zurich, hot-dip galvanized in the surrounding area, and finally covered by hand with 150 meters of plastic cord. Who invented it? Exactly!

Not only should you listen to Italians when they speak, you should watch them as well. Their sweeping gestures and the range of their nonverbal communication are simply unrivaled. Studies have identified a striking difference in the speech of people from northern and southern European countries in terms of what parts of their bodies are involved: Germans apparently gesture more from the wrist, Italians from the shoulder or elbow. In any case, the people on the other side of the Alps seem to have a much more expansive approach when it comes to emphasizing their own words. Star architect Aldo Rossi was typically Italian in this respect as well and not at all minimalist when it came to literal speech. Only in his work did he cultivate the art of reduction. Rossi became involved in Alessi's famous Tea & Coffee Piazza project in 1984. As part of the project, Alessi had invited 11 prominent architects to each design a silver tea and coffee set. Rossi delivered designs that broke down the gabled roofs, towers, domes, and columns of an Italian cityscape into the simplest geometric shapes: triangles, semicircles, cubes. The result, among other things, was the La Conica espresso pot.

Aldo Rossi | 1989

La Cupola

The Rossi and Alessi families grew closer as a result of the project, and they've been pretty much best friends ever since. Regarding his friend's design language, company founder Alberto Alessi once said, "He just didn't believe in the saying: form follows function." Alessi also revealed that he was the one who had asked Aldo Rossi for another espresso maker: In his opinion, La Conica was too expensive and impractical. As a result, Rossi created the cast aluminum La Cupola version in 1989—clearly more functional and four times cheaper than its big sister. Both are straightforward and precise; Rossi, economical as he was, did not add a single unnecessary line to his sketch. He beautifully presented his design in a drawing depicting La Cupola as a structure adjacent to an Italian Renaissance building. Unusual to see a coffee pot in an urban cityscape? You should take a look at the Bonnefantenmuseum in Maastricht. The resemblance is striking. The architect: Aldo Rossi. Who else?

30

Almost sacral in appearance:
the espresso-making coffee pot La Cupola.

George Nelson | 1956

Marshmallow Sofa

Borrowed plumes can sometimes be very flattering. The crow was well aware of this when he found iridescent peacock feathers on the ground and proudly added them to his own plumage. He probably could have pranced around like that undisturbed for quite some time, but he went too far and strutted straight through a group of peacocks. They not only plucked out the borrowed plumes but also the crow's own feathers. At least that's the story as told by the Roman author Phaedrus. It's a fable, of course, a lesson meant to make us wiser, and in this case warn us. And it gave us the wonderful saying: Don't adorn yourself with borrowed plumes.

Irving Harper would agreed. He was employed as a creative by the New York studio belonging to design great George Nelson, who for his part was working for the furniture manufacturer Herman Miller. On his own time and without compensation, Harper had already designed the company logo. He just happened to be standing there in 1954 when a sales representative for plastic products was promoting round foam cushions. Nelson was attracted more by the low price than by the objects themselves and asked Harper to design a piece of furniture around them. Harper tinkered over a weekend, draped a steel frame with 18 of these discs, and created the Marshmallow sofa. It was covered with fabric, vinyl, or leather, came in brilliant colors, and had a great deal of star appeal. Under the Herman Miller label and officially designed by George Nelson, it came onto the market in 1956, with Harper's name only appearing on the bottom of the steel frame. No one questioned the sofa's authorship and colorful spheres had been part of Nelson's characteristic style since his Ball Clock in 1950.

In the end, the smart sofa idea left the company holding the bag, all because of filthy lucre. Because each of the 18 cushions had to be covered by hand, the cost of manufacturing the sofa was much more than expected. By the time it was withdrawn from the market in 1961, only 186 had been sold for $15,000 a piece. But none of the buyers would have reason to complain about the high price. In 2000, one of the originals was auctioned off at Sotheby's for €37,500.

And Harper? At some point he left the company and went on to design various pieces, but his name never stuck to any of them. Meanwhile, his sofa was reissued by Vitra—for connoisseurs, naturally. You can demonstrate your own connoisseurship by searching out Harper's signature on the frame. Yes, George Nelson, borrowed plumes can be so beautiful—and delightfully colorful.

Quirky, colorful and amazingly comfortable: the Marshmallow Sofa is a real eye-catcher!

31

Elegant yet playful: The Snoopy lamp makes a good eye-catcher, but can also be a team player—for example on the Laccio table, designed by Marcel Breuer (▶ p. 145).

Surveys have shown that people in neighboring countries consider Germans to be without a sense of humor. A Swiss newspaper recently postulated that Germans lack the tradition of French comedy, the Englishman's cheerful understatement in everyday things, and the Jewish ability to crack jokes in the face of despair. That really is no grounds for merriment, and, indeed, there are quite a lot of things to laugh about in the land between the Alps and the North Sea.

What Germans lack, perhaps, is a certain lightness of spirit, which makes a sense of humor much easier. It may even be refreshing to apply a kind of intellectual wit to a serious study of jokes, fun, and laughter itself. And so scientists have examined the language of Mickey Mouse, analyzed Donald Duck and—no joke!—examined "biodiversity in Duck Tales." The latter is a subject that fun-loving pranksters should certainly take seriously. Zan Owlson, Storkules, and Nicky the neurotic nightingale have all turned up in Donald Duck's comic universe.

Californian psychologist James C. Kaufman, who had various *Peanuts* characters on his couch, draws some interesting conclusions. He diagnosed neuroticism in Charlie Brown, patterns of aggressive behavior in Lucy, a tendency toward intellectual reflection in Linus. He found Snoopy to be adventurous and always about to put his foot into it, an extreme extrovert. Of course, he is also a grandstander and daydreamer. Sometimes he thinks he is a flying ace in the First World War, then a world-famous ice-skating champion. He is always ready to show his stuff on a skateboard. His alter ego is Joe Cool. Can you really take comic characters seriously? They don't actually exist. They are a figment of someone's imagination. Indeed, what is reality after all? Could it just be a collective dream? We have now truly spoiled the fun. Entire generations of literati have namely worked through the question.

Achille and Pier Giacomo Castiglioni | 1967

Snoopy

It is simply a fact that our imaginations help determine our reality, since every human endeavor began as an idea in a person's mind.

And sometimes real-life objects turn right around and return to the imaginary world. For example, real design classics sometimes turn up in comic books: a chair by Mies van der Rohe in *The Adventures of Tintin*, the Butterfly Chair in Charlie Brown's bedroom from *Peanuts*, and the Taccia lamp by Achille Castiglioni, which illuminates the Italian animation series *Diabolik*. You could even say it is enhanced reality. Maybe it is proof that comic book authors and designers are on the same wavelength, a topic that the Vitra Design Museum felt was worth exploring in its 2019 *Living in a Box* exhibit. The latter dealt with icons that entered imaginary worlds, but this migration is equally entertaining in the opposite direction. The Ikea furniture empire reconstructed the *Simpsons'* living room for an ad campaign in Saudi Arabia with the caption "For real families." The Italian designer Achille Castiglioni would have found this amusing. He never had any use for people who take themselves too seriously. "Irony is important. In design. In every object," he once said. "One of my secrets is that I am always joking around!" He approached design with tongue planted firmly in cheek. Not only did he turn a tractor seat into a stool, he also created installations from toilet bowls. His Arco lamp is evidence that he had no fear of being trite. He drilled a hole into the heavy marble base and initially paired each piece with a broom. This allowed you to insert the broom into the hole in the marble and use the heavy lamp to sweep the floor.

In 1967, he also gave the Snoopy table lamp designed with his brother Pier Giacomo a marble base, which lent it stability, helped it rest firmly on the tabletop, and provided a counterweight to the piece's enormous head. Three things that would not have suited his source of inspiration, the recalcitrant beagle from *Peanuts*. After all, the animal was always slightly off his rocker, presumably the very attribute that Castiglioni loved the most about him when he based this successful design on the dog. The reason why he named the lamp Snoopy needs no explanation. All you have to do is look at it. It perfectly exemplifies Castiglioni's credo: "Delete, delete, delete and in the end, find the core aspect of the design." The lamp only hints at Snoopy's form, and yet he is unmistakeable. Joe Cool on the sideboard instead of his skateboard. Brilliant!

A couple of years ago, a 19-year-old Canadian tossed a chair out of the window on the 45th floor of a skyscraper in Toronto. This may not have been her most brilliant idea. The fact that she took a video of her action, captioned it "Good Morning," and then posted it on the Internet was even less brilliant. Her energetic early-morning performance landed her in court—and it cost her dearly. People who throw chairs about are usually not at their best. They are falling-down drunk, off their rockers, or are at the end of their rope and therefore best left alone. It is an especially bad idea to place other pieces of furniture in their way. A shrewd attorney might have even gotten his 19-year-old client out of her fix by mentioning a famous role model. In 1957, architect Giovanni "Gio" Ponti threw a chair onto the street from the fourth-floor window of an apartment building. He wanted to see whether his newly created Superleggera chair would withstand the impact in an effort to test its limits. A bit far-fetched? In fact, it's not any more brutal that pounding a chair with many tons of mechanical force, as many furniture-makers do.

Giovanni Ponti | 1951

Superleggera

The Superleggera suffered a few scratches but otherwise withstood the experiment without further damage. At 1.7 kilograms, the lightweight proved to be a tough customer and therefore had the right stuff. Ponti expected nothing less of the "one true chair" he believed to have ever designed. He described his elegant creation as a "just a chair without adjectives," which wasn't exactly true. After all, Superleggera means "super-lightweight" in Italian. Ponti based his first version on the traditional and dirt-cheap chairs that had been produced in the fishing village of Chiavari, Liguria, since the 19th century. He reduced its form to the bare necessities, worked an ergonomic curve into the seat back, and in doing so hit the nail on the head. Somehow, the maestro must have fallen victim to a kind of anorexia, because he slimmed it down even further with the aid of connecting straps and ash wood. Until the chair became a featherweight at less than two kilos, and thus a flying object. Indeed, the name, Superleggera, places Signore Ponti's young charge in the best of company. High-performance vehicles, such as Maserati, Ferrari, and Lamborghini, have added this attribute to their own names, which describes a particularly complex design in the manufacture of car bodies. Superleggera is therefore not just an adjective, it is an aristocratic title.

The name says it all: The chair made of very light ash wood weighs just 1,700 grams.

33

Enzo Mari | 1963

Uno, la mela

Have you ever looked at Joseph Beuys' famous felt suit and wondered, bewildered, why on earth it is considered art? In fact, the artist actually made a statement with his two-piece suit: Felt keeps you warm and helps against the cold, even the kind that comes from fighters in war. Sometimes even a genius has to explain himself, otherwise he is easily misjudged. Martin Kippenberger's installation in Dortmund's Museum Ostwall, for example, fell victim to confusion with a mundane everyday object: A cleaning woman scrubbed away the deposit in the bottom of the rubber tub that belonged to the installation—unfortunately, that deposit was precisely what the work was all about, as revealed by the title "Wenn's anfängt, durch die Decke zu tropfen" (When It Starts Dripping From the Ceiling). The damages: 800,000 euros. On the other hand, a prankster at the Guggenheim Museum simply hung his own work among the big names, which nobody noticed for quite some time.

We have learned that art is in the eye of the beholder, and in the case of Enzo Mari's nature drawings from the 1960s, we need to be gracious in our assessment. We see an apple and a pear, a frog, a pig, a panther, and other motifs from rural life, and they honestly don't differ much from the little wooden boards that are used in a nursery school to mark individual groups, for example. They could also decorate a picture book. But perhaps that's precisely where the stroke of genius can be found?

"To think simply is a gift from God. To think simply and to speak simply is a two-fold gift from God." This was said by Konrad Adenauer, and if we extend "speak simply" to also mean "express simply," then perhaps we can include paintings, and with that Mari would be vindicated. "An apple is not an apple, it's the apple," the designer once philosophized, meaning that there is only one perfect form for a thing, and it usually succeeds in nature and nowhere else. The images that Mari made of animals and fruits stylize what nature once dictated, breaking down the natural form into its essence. For Mari, greatness was expressed in simplicity. In his opinion, the ball was the perfect object: purism pure and simple, and an object that everyone could relate to.

Throughout his creative years, Mari practiced asceticism when it came to basic forms. He designed office materials, children's games, vases, and the first DIY furniture—19 chairs, tables, and beds that were simple to assemble and whose blueprints he sent to anyone who sent him a stamped envelope. He hated the elite pretensions of design, and instead created beauty for the masses. "I work for factories, not for boutiques," he said; he wanted everyone to be able to afford his art. Even back then, he attached great importance to sustainability: "When I design an object, it has to last at least 100 years, or better yet 1,000 years." Simple things for people, with a claim to eternity—the common denominator has to be as large as possible, and the object itself as simple as possible. And that explains the apple, the pear, the panther.

Mari died of COVID-19 in 2020, and he bequeathed his archive to the city of Milan. In the next four decades, the city will gain little more from it than the storage costs. Mari's condition for his bequest was clear: It has to remain under lock and key for forty years, because he felt that the design world was not ready for it. After all, his apple graphic, along with his other naive drawings, is already out in the wild, on its way to immortality. It already has more than half a century under its belt. But it always seems fresh. Good enough to eat, you might say.

Charles and Ray Eames | 1956

Lounge Chair

The design world has produced an astonishing number of successful partnerships. Mixed doubles appearing in photos or on a brand's website make a good impression. It isn't just the table or chair they've designed that attracts people, it's their creative alliance. But whether the creative process between these two people proceeds like a harmonious pas de deux is another thing entirely. Many couples break out in a sweat when they imagine having to spend both their personal and professional lives constantly in each other's company. And yet it seems to work: Yael Mer and Shay Alkalay, Neri & Hu, Eva Marguerre and Marcel Besau—although the husband-and-wife team of Stefan Scholten and Carole Baijings did throw in the towel after a 19-year partnership, calling an end to their colorful collaboration in 2019. By contrast, spouses Charles and Ray Eames, design icons of the 20th century, appear to have been true believers in "till death do us part." Every day they wrote each other little notes whose contents might appear on WhatsApp today. And isn't it so much more romantic to take pen in hand and write a few loving words to your significant other that come

„Why don't we make a contemporary version
of the old English club chair?"

straight from your soul? The Eames not only worked together but they also liked to take their work home with them—for example, to experiment with plywood—and when they dined with friends, they never tired of discussing the art of living. One day, director Billy Wilder happened to be sitting at their table, one of a number friends that Charles had made as a set designer in Hollywood. Wilder was complaining about the fact that when he was in the middle of an exhausting shoot, he had no comfortable chair where he could take a quick nap. He was considering getting an English club chair, but at the word "comfortable," a different picture spontaneously formed in the minds of both Eames: "a well-used first baseman's mitt." The follow-up was an artistic combination of the best of two worlds and a masterpiece that's still unmatched today: the famous Eames lounge chair. This particular piece of furniture marked the first time that Charles and Ray set aside their principle of affordable and mass-producible. With its aluminum frame and cushions embedded in a plywood shell, the lounge chair was fairly expensive to manufacture. As a luxury item—still produced today by hand in a 47-step process—it's the equivalent of a compact car. Need an example? When French President François Hollande compelled his ministers to disclose their assets in 2013, the Minister of Industry listed two objects as his most valuable possessions: his Peugeot and his Eames chair.

Although there's no real reason to alter a good design, the lounge chair has undergone several modifications—not because of the chair itself but because of us. People are getting bigger, so the chair has also had to put on an additional ten centimeters.

Billy Wilder napped on the prototype at its original height of 84 centimeters. He also got a very good deal: The Eames gave him the chair as a gift.

A couple who set the pace: Charles and Ray Eames are among the most successful designer couples in history.

Let's talk about love. At this point, most people would likely emit a rapturous sigh, lose themselves in the most blissful of dreams, and babble on incoherently while carried away on a cloud of intense emotions. But let's take a more rational approach to the matter, a scientific one, in fact. Whatever the turbulent state of our emotions, the reason is always a biochemical one and follows neurobiological patterns aimed at only one thing: reproduction. Heart all a flutter, blushing, etc., none of these sensations take place anywhere in our breast but happen quite simply in the brain. Slide a person in love into the MRI scanner and you will be struck by the unmistakeable fact that their limbic reward system is in a state of constant stress. Passionate love resembles addiction, and the body mixes a hormone cocktail that is a veritable a witches' brew. It has caused many a woman to throw herself at the feet of some ne-er-do-well, and many a man to shower his beloved with roses, rings, and proclamations of undying adoration. Sometimes it even drives them to madness. After all, the Taj Mahal in India stands witness to the power of boundless earthly love, even if the adored Mumtaz Mahal never had time to enjoy it. Unfortunately, the magnificent palace that Shah Jahan built for his adored wife became her mausoleum. Nevertheless, the two love-birds were able to share a blissful existence for quite some time, since Mumtaz Mahal died giving birth to the couple's fourteenth child.

Piero Fornasetti | 1950s

Tema e Variazioni

It's also true that passion can grow if you gaze upon the object of your desire only from a distance. The artist Piero Fornasetti is excellent proof of this. From the moment he laid eyes on the portrait of the legendary Italian soprano Lina Cavalieri in a 1950s magazine, he was so taken by her countenance that he had ever new versions of it printed on chess boards, lampshades, furniture, and plates. Albeit in ways that might not have always been pleasing to her. Once he painted her with a clown's nose, another time with a moustache. He covered her entire face with adhesive tape, had a monster hang from her mouth, placed a diver's helmet over her pretty little head, and tied it up with string like a package. The five husbands that Signora Cavalieri went through in her lifetime, as well as her long string of admirers, whom she regularly rebuffed, might have indulged in a certain malicious satisfaction in seeing Fornasetti's fantasies. Nevertheless, the singer ranks only fourth among the world's most frequently painted women in the history of art, after the Virgin Mary, Cleopatra, and Marchesa Luisa Casati, who ate men for breakfast and strolled about Rome at the turn of the turn of the twentieth century, preferably leading a baby crocodile on a leash. Still, fame is everything.

The legend lives on, making sure that other people can also profit from her fame. After Fornasetti's death in 1988, his son, Barnaba, followed in his father's admiring footsteps and added a pilot's goggles and a woolen balaclava to the singer's visage. After all, love has many faces.

36

Eclectic Italian: The Fornasetti series includes over 150 different wall plates.

FAILURE OR NOT?
An idea to die for. But unfortunately, the sofa often melted before it was put to use.

37

Fall down, stand up, straighten your crown, and carry on. Whether this postcard saying really gives comfort in moments when you are lying on the ground with bruised knees is something I dare to doubt. Actually, in Germany, those who have fallen have a particularly hard time getting back on their feet. Industrial psychologists describe the way that Germans deal with errors and defeats as not constructive at all. Only Singapore seems to be worse off in that matter. Yet almost all successful ideas are based on the pas de deux of trial and error. "Success is the exception," technology historian Reinhold Bauer summed it up, "failure is the rule." What's more, anyone who achieves great things also sometimes falls flat on their face.

Marcus Engman | 1980s

Air

This also happened to Marcus Engman, Ikea's head of design at the time. During a cheerful brainstorming session the ideas flew across the conference table like ping-pong balls, and somehow they all fell in love with the concept of an inflatable sofa. The idea wasn't completely out of the blue; there were, after all, respectable competitors, such as the Blow chair by Jonathan de Pas, Donato D'Urbino and Paolo Lomazzi from 1967 (▶ p. 218). They assured each other of the genius of such a sofa, "one of those special moments when we call Eureka," Engman later recalled. The thing, which fit into a fruit crate—thus paying tribute to Ikea's take-home philosophy—and which the buyer could conveniently inflate with a hair dryer at home, went into series production in the mid-1980s. And that's when disaster struck: Ikea had forgotten to mention in the instruction manual that it was better to set the hair dryer to cold air before inflating. And if the Ikea Air was finally filled to the brim in the living room, it was so light that it constantly moved around. Also, the sofas kept losing air: "We compared them to swollen hippos," Engman said in an interview. "They moved around the room and were flatter on Fridays than on Mondays. They also made unpleasant noises when you sat on them." So the Ikea Air's success either melted away or was extremely volatile. A pity really.

Engman, who has a strong hereditary background at Ikea—his father had been head of development there, his mother had been marketing manager, and his sister worked for corporate communications—took it with humor, tinkered with the teething troubles, tried with better valves, pimped the airhead in the 2000s in a last attempt at a children's sofa, but at some point the air was just out—in every respect. At the Democratic Design Days in Sydney, a conference that he himself had initiated, he confessed that the Ikea Air was one of the biggest mistakes in Ikea's history, a downright grandiose fiasco. And he was proud to have been involved in it.

After all, failure is part of the process. Engman, who founded his own consulting firm in 2018 but continues to work with Ikea, understood that. As probably all truly creative minds in this world.

The British say "against all odds" when someone wins the race who actually had no chance. It's something that happens in sports every now and then—such as in the case of Pastorius, a horse that ran so poorly in the run-up to the 2012 Deutsches Derby that his owner actually wanted to withdraw him from the race shortly before the start—and then, astonishingly, he won. Or the miracle of Bern in 1954, when Germany unexpectedly won the FIFA World Cup. And let's face it, it wasn't exactly obvious that Cinderella would upstage her gussied-up sisters and make off with the prince. Does the unexpected often happen? Not really. Most things take a fairly predictable course—which is why betting on outsiders is so lucrative.

Even the wooden molar was initially somewhat ridiculed as a furniture innovation; after all, it was really just a waste product. When the heartwood legs of the best-selling dining table from the e15 design label were sawed, leftover pieces always fell off, and that really annoyed designer Philipp Mainzer—he hates it when his favorite natural material goes to waste. He picked up the oak offcuts, fine-tuned them in the London factory, and finally combined four of each into a stool. Don't ever let anything go to waste—Mainzer was spot-on when it came to sustainability. In 1996, he lugged his prototype onto a plane to Hamburg in his carry-on bag, where the bag was entrusted to its very own flight attendant. The stewardess took care of it because it didn't fit in the overhead compartment above Mainzer's seat or under the seat in front of him (it's a good thing Mainzer apparently hadn't decided to fly Ryanair or one of the other budget airlines). On his return flight, the designer left his 15-kilogram companion behind; several Hamburg designer furniture stores had become so enamored with it that the newcomer was immediately adopted by the Hanseatic city. And Mainzer returned home with a fistful of orders in hand.

The molar with its integrated recessed seat is still a youngster, of course, having just outgrown its infancy, but somehow the stool is already a real classic. You could jokingly say that it's a piece with teeth, but it would be far more fitting to say that it's a stool with a crack. The crack is part of it, a quality feature, so to speak, because during the storage of the solid wood, these indentations are formed, which make each one of these furniture minis a character piece. Perhaps as a seating group at the dining table from which they are directly descended? There you go! It never hurts to show some teeth!

Philipp Mainzer | 1996

Molar Stool

Not simply a stool, but a structure made of four legs so massive that they form the seat at the same time.

38

Most of us have loved building blocks since our early childhood. With Lego bricks you could become the creator of your own worlds, and at that time the plastic cuboids really stimulated the imagination: Generations of children used them to build houses, cars, towers, the bricks did it all. The name Lego from the Danish "leg godt", play well, worked really well. Since 1949 and for decades after, the bricks were the big hit, pedagogically the finest for creativity or fine motor skills, and in terms of spatial imagination, they taught more than many geometry lessons. At that time, they were also still politically correct and unsuspicious, which of course changed with the concentration on the themed sets, because from then on, criticism and the zeitgeist struck: Sometimes they were considered too violence-loving, sometimes the figures were too sexist and not diverse enough. And the construction kit became somehow also rather unfashionable. In the past, we poured out bags of bricks and then decided what we wanted to build; today, instructions usually tell us which part belongs on top of the other.

Fritz Haller | 1963

USM Haller

Things were definitely more consistent at USM Haller. For 60 years, the company has been making in building sets, admittedly in a completely different league. However, the inventor of the ingenious system did not initially have domestic use in mind, but rather the big picture: In 1961, architect Fritz Haller was commissioned by company heir Paul Schärer to build a new roof over the head of the family business, which had started out as a locksmith's store in 1885 and in the meantime was producing window fittings and various hardware. Haller designed a structure that was held in place by steel frames—and because it was so beautiful, he also built the Schärers' private house in the same style on a steep slope in the swiss landscape, a modern dream home with a panoramic view, the so-called Buchli.

These sideboards bring order to life,
and color too.

Two years later, when Haller was asked to create a furniture series for the factory and offices, he reverted to the tried-and-tested look: metal side panels, shelves and covers were held in place by chrome tubes, turning every filing cabinet and container in the building into a "box in the box", so to speak. The highlight of the system, which could be used to make tables, cabinets and sideboards, only became apparent to the observer at second glance: an elegant steel ball connected the chrome rods.

Naturally, the futuristic new building and its interior made it into a design magazine, and it was there that the Rothschild Bank in Paris discovered it and ordered the system on a grand scale. The rest is history: Sideboard & Co. went into series production and moved from the offices into the private spheres of their fans. And, incidentally, also into the museum: as applied art, a USM-Haller sideboard can also be found in New York's MoMA. In Münsingen, Switzerland, the company has since been proving on a daily basis in the production of the individual parts for its famous modular system that a steel ball hail does not necessarily have to have martial features—but can have a decidedly unifying character.

A constructive triad of sphere, tube and surface: Fritz Haller developed a system that has lost none of its aesthetic timelessness to this day.

The Knotted Chair is knotted as a net, soaked in synthetic resin and then simply hung up to dry.

106   Chair

Marcel Wanders | 1996
Knotted Chair

Knots are usually intended to solve problems. They connect what wouldn't stay together on its own, and they give structure and support to individual threads. The famous Gordian knot in particular was known for its extreme intricacy that was seemingly impossible to untangle. According to Greek legend, after Gordias was declared king, his son Midas tied the ox-cart to a post using a knot so intricate it defied numerous attempts to unravel it. An oracle proclaimed that the person to untie it was destined to rule all of Asia. Until finally Alexander the Great drew his sword and cut the knot, stopping the king in his tracks, and going on to conquer Asia. It seemed like a bit of a shortcut given that it should be possible to use the power of the mind to untangle knots. German mathematical genius Kurt Reidemeister, for instance, used algebra in an attempt to unravel these elaborate structures. Knots, clearly, are both an art and a skill.

The International Guild of Knot Tyers quite rightly takes a bow to inventive minds who come up with ingenious new types of knots. The most recent member to achieve immortality was a certain Bob Daniel in 1989 with the Daniel harness knot. By the way, the fact that there are now around 4000 knots listed is not due to eager guild members, but rather to the many bored sailors in the 19th century who passed their time during periods of calm by constantly experimenting with new ways of knotting the ropes. On top of that, the Crusaders brought back a number of knots from the Orient, including the macramé technique, which was later used to make tapestries and hammocks in Europe.

In 1996, it seems unlikely that designer Marcel Wanders tried his hand at tying the knots he needed just for the fun of it. It is more likely that he simply enjoyed experimenting in all kinds of ways: Using every trick in the book, he used knots to create a net of coated carbon fibers, which are usually used to make bulletproof vests. He then dipped it in epoxy resin, and hung it up in a wooden frame to dry. Gravity took care of the rest. Gravity sometimes doesn't do us any favors when we're growing older, but in this case it didn't ruin any contours—in fact, it helped shape the chair, which went down in design history as the Knotted Chair. "It was like a minor miracle," Wanders later recalled, overjoyed. He added: "It's a chair that tells you it's made just for you with a great deal of love, creativity, and care. A chair that has an individual and personal touch, a chair that shows its connection to you by revealing new details as often as you use it." Note that you may be able to create nets and apparently even chairs with knots, but it is with words that you weave the legend to go along with it.

It all began with a draining rack and ended as a universal shelf: String from 1949 by Kajsa and Nils Strinning.

The fact that single men do more around the house than married men should give one pause. And yet, according to a study by the University of Michigan, women find their workload doubled once they tie the knot. However, when men and women divide up their housecleaning chores fairly, they are 50% more likely to divorce, according to Norwegian statisticians. The researchers speculate that people in such balanced marriages have a predilection to discuss everything, and these discussions tent to end in bitter disputes. In the last century, at least, this was not a problem, if only because the division of work was clearly defined. Most women had a narrowly delineated sphere of influence, and the lady of the house most definitely did not ask her spouse to help out by doing the dishes. Instead, she would rather have her lord and master buy her some new gadget for her kitchen. In the 1940s, for example, a whole lot of companies then competed with each other to invent the best such appliances. After the war, Germany set about rebuilding the country, and as things progressed, it became clear that the number of people who could afford fine furniture was not enough to drive the economy. Instead, the masses had to be taught the art of consumerism, and this required affordable products. An idea developed by architecture student Nils Strinning was just the thing. He had invented a dishrack that could be mounted on the wall next to the sink, and he presented it to a relative who worked for Elfa, a purveyor of household goods. The state-run Hemmets forskningsinstitut, whose team of experts dedicated themselves to making life easier for the Swedish housewife, put on the finishing touches. The dishrack went into successful mass production. This gave young Nisse, as he was called, a wonderful foot in the door of the business, for of course, by now, the lad had tasted blood. One day, while sitting on the toilet, it occurred to him that the plastic-coated wire rack could perhaps do even more than simply help out in the kitchen. Just fashion the wire into a mini-ladder and a support for a couple of wooden boards and presto, you had a splendid shelf. The very thing that the publishing house Bonnier was looking for in a 1949 design competition. Not only did it have to accommodate two meters of books, it also had to be folded up quickly and easily into a thin package and be endlessly expandable. Strinning's String seemed to be the answer to the questions of the day. The young architect had scored a real coup. Bingo.

Kajsa and Nils „Nisse" Strinning | 1949

String Shelf

The product embarked on an unparalleled victory march. Everyone in Sweden got one, the shelf was installed at the United Nations headquarters in New York, and even in Germany people flocked to the latticed shelf in droves. It became the bestselling piece of Scandinavian furniture. When Bonnier discontinued production in 1971, Nils and his wife Karin bought back their design, so to speak. It wasn't until 2005 that the String returned to the market, now having grown into a whole family. To mark the revival, Nisse himself designed the String Pocket, a kind of mini-version, which has long since become a bestseller. The shelf was officially pronounced an art object in 2009, while Sweden put it on postage stamps in 2017. Unfortunately, Nils and Karin were no longer able to celebrate this success together, since they had divorced in 1978. Do you think they shared their housework and perhaps discussed it too many times? We'll never know.

We really need to talk about women. In the history of design, there is a tendency to sweep women under the carpet—bear with us, we had to use this metaphor since it fits so nicely with the subject. Ray and Charles Eames not only shared a bed, of course, but many successes as well—but give some thought to the Corbusier Lounge Chair. By the great master Le Corbusier? He was only too happy to perpetuate this myth. It was in fact Charlotte Perriand, while in her mid-twenties, who designed the expensive piece in 1928 while working as one of Le Corbusier's partners in his Paris architectural firm. The iconic String bookshelf by Nils "Nisse" Strinning was probably more of a collaborative design with his wife, Karin, or "Kajsa." Even the Bauhaus, which was one of the very first teaching establishments to accept women into its simple but sacred walls, subsequently tended to treat them as second-class citizens. Its founder Walter Gropius, who had initially advocated for the inclusion of women, was convinced that women could only think two-dimensionally—and thus sent the female students to work in the in-house weaving mill. There they were expected to stay firmly in their place since there was little else for them to do.

Lilly Reich and Ludwig Mies van der Rohe | 1929

Barcelona Chair

By contrast, the third Bauhaus director, Ludwig Mies van der Rohe—born in Aachen as Maria Ludwig Michael Mies—had a deep appreciation for his collaborations with his partner, Lilly Reich. That said, although they worked together on numerous projects, she remained in the shadows. It is said that they collaborated on the planning of the German Pavilion at the 1929 World's Fair. For their showpiece, the pair of chairs that would later go down in design history as the Barcelona Chairs, Ludwig and Lilly drew inspiration from the scissor chairs upon which caesars, emperors, and kings used to sit. This was probably no coincidence, because the chairs were expecting high-profile guests: The Spanish royal couple, Alfonso and Victoria, were expected to sit on them during the opening ceremony of the pavilion. Whether they did or not is not known for sure. If not, they might have been annoyed, since it would have gone down in history.

After the exhibition, the chair was first produced in Berlin and Bamberg, then at Thonet, and later in Chicago and New York—it became a global player, after all. Knoll International has been making the chair since 1964, and the chrome-plated

Designed for the German Pavilion at the 1929 World's Fair in Barcelona.

stainless steel continues to be polished to a mirror finish by hand just as it has always been. In 2014, the chair's upholstery was beefed up significantly, and its users now seem to have become a bit spoiled.

"It's almost easier to build a skyscraper than a chair," Mies van der Rohe is reported to have once said. Van der Rohe designed the Barcelona Chair, the Brno Chair, and the Weißenhof Chair, but Lilly is rarely credited as the originator. But some historians suspect that she was the one who came up with the ideas in the first place. Albert Pfeiffer, Vice President of Design and Management at Knoll, is an expert on Reich. His belief: "It became more than a coincidence that Mies's involvement and success in exhibition design began at the same time as his personal relationship with Reich." It had to be said.

The Barcelona Chair is considered one of the most important furniture designs of modernism. On the right, one of its creators, Ludwig Mies van der Rohe.

Egon Eiermann | 1953
E1 Desk

Sometime during the 1990s, I fell in love. The object of my affection was called R2-D2, a droid with an attitude. He was my favorite hero in *Star Wars*, and the only reason he never reciprocated my feelings was because he was a robot who couldn't comprehend human emotions. His name was a reflection of his mechanical essence but gave no clue to the fact that it originated in the high society of Hollywood greats. It was invented by the sound engineer for *King Kong* and *Citizen Kane*, who called the second dialog track on the second reel of film R-2 D-2 (Reel 2, Dialog 2). His son Richard Portman later used this same abbreviation when mixing *The Godfather*, until it was finally picked up by his extremely busy colleague Walter Murch. Right after the filming of *Star Wars* began, Murch was mixing the sound for *American Graffiti* and mumbled something about R2 D2 while he was labeling the tracks. George Lucas overheard him and loved it so much that it became the droid's name. I don't know what the story is behind the name of his pal C-3PO. What I do know is that letter-number combinations are also very popular among other creative types. The design world is full of mysterious abbreviations: Wegner's CH24 chair, Thonet's S 64 version, Eileen Gray's E 1027 table. We can't exactly accuse good designers of a lack of imagination, so it's all the more surprising that they give their precious works names that sound more like the code on a truck-stop or Chinese restaurant menu. "One B 12, please" is much easier to say than "one Mandarin-style duck with rice and spring rolls, not too spicy."

The original E1 Desk frame was designed in 1953 by Egon Eiermann at Karlsruhe University for his students.

43

So does E2 say it all? It at least identifies the desk as a piece of German functionalism, the "Second Modernity," more uniquely than calling it an "Eiermann." It's simply a steel-tube frame with a white melamine top and beech wood edge bands. As a bustling architect, Egon Eiermann had many irons in the fire. In the 1960s, he designed an innovative coffin for transporting bodies on airplanes for the Grieneisen funeral home in Berlin. He also demolished the famous Schocken Department Store building by Erich Mendelsohn despite massive protests and replaced it with a plain Horten box. In 1937, he hung an 18-meter-tall portrait of Hitler on the exhibition hall near the Berlin Radio Tower for the propaganda exhibition "Give me four years time." And in 1953, he invented this simple desk for his own use—employing metal, by the way—and his students at the Karlsruhe Institute of Technology (KIT) were so taken with it that they developed a limited series for the school's drawing classrooms. At that point, the frame wasn't yet collapsible, but when Eiermann's assistant Klaus Brunner moved to Freiburg twelve years later, he asked whether a more portable version could be made. Adam Wieland, head of the metal workshop at KIT, came up with the clever idea of making the crossbars foldable and screwing the side components together instead of welding them. Starting in the late 1990s, the entrepreneur Richard Lampert began producing this slightly modified original, which underwent another complete revision in 2009. Since then, it carries its modernity in its name: E2—sometimes the best approach is to keep it simple, stupid. And the E2 actually wears its conciseness well. After all, it was created to be a worker bee, not a diva.

In the 1960s, the frame became foldable—by fixing the intersecting rods with screws.

Charles and Ray Eames | 1950
Plastic Chair

Are good designs always a little stuck-up? That's a preconception that's already perching on every expensive chair before an admirer can even sit on it and fills the space around the big-name tables—where it has no business being. The creative geniuses responsible for these works never had any intention of using their designs to stuff their pockets full of cash. Many of them just wanted to make the world a slightly better place. That sounds like a naive cliché, like starry-eyed idealism that deserves to be met with a little skepticism. But behind every design is a basic idea, and these ideas were surprisingly public-spirited during the decades of mid-century modern design. In 1947, for example, Italian designer Enzo Mari created a series of furnishings that his fans could build themselves from materials purchased at their local hardware store—probably the world's first do-it-yourself icons. In the post-war years, Denmark was eagerly crafting its Social State. And because good design is practically a Scandinavian birthright, great masters like Arne Jacobsen and Hans J. Wegner were hurrying to design mass-producible furniture that anyone could afford. Social consciousness was a central theme in modernism and functionalism to such an extent that it would be hard to imagine the architecture without it. Economical materials and production methods in particular helped bring these good intentions to fruition.

In faraway America, as well, there was concern for the aesthetic awareness of those who had no money to spare. Lord knows, Charles and Ray Eames didn't set out to create iconic designs for society just so they could end up in the houses of the rich and famous. Most of what they made was initially for themselves, basically for their own use, but their motto was always, "The best for the most for the least." Their famous plastic chair, however, has a very special history. In 1948, the couple entered a chair with a seat shell made of stamped metal in the New York Museum of Modern Art's "International Competition for Low-Cost Furniture Design." This chair was extremely heavy, making it impractical and certainly not award-worthy. For their second attempt, they chose polyester resin, which was used to reinforce fiberglass. Until then, this material had at most served to cover radar equipment or was used experimentally in aircraft construction and shipbuilding. It was perfect for the Eames' purposes: easy to mold, sturdy, and very cheap.

The chair entered mass production in 1950 just as they intended. It found its way into schools, cafeterias, offices, and universities and became a universal object that anyone could own. Starting in 1957, it was manufactured by Herman Miller and Vitra and, in the early 2000s after a mere ten-year break, was relaunched with a shell made of the more ecofriendly material polypropylene. It's still an icon, although a relatively pricy one—through no fault of the design or of its designers.

45

Petra Hesser, former head of Ikea's German operations, doesn't exactly give men a good report card. When it comes to assembling furniture, she recognized some fundamental weaknesses among them: "Because men never look at the instructions, they have the most problems during assembly because they always think they can do it," she said, referring to empirical research. Do it yourself? Clearly with some limitations.

The do-it-yourself movement emerged in the 1950s in the wake of the Arts and Crafts Movement in England. In the 1960s and 1970s, it gave expression to thoroughly political elements: self-empowerment, personal initiative, distrust of industry. DIY was thus the natural enemy of furniture companies.

Nevertheless, it was by sheer coincidence and not by design that Ikea invented the DIY "light" movement, so to speak, in 1978. Originally the fourth employee to join the company in 1953, having been hired to look after the Ikea catalog, Gillis Lundgren became one of the longest-serving designers. Decades later, he wanted to ship a coffee table and came to the conclusion that it was a damned unwieldy business. He made some initial sketches on paper napkins while eating, so it stands to reason that at some point between meatballs and potatoes, he reconsidered the dimensions of the package and essentially started playing Tetris on paper, as it were. He quickly found the solution to his problem: He unscrewed the legs from the table and placed them in the package together with the table top. He had solved his problem—and in passing had invented self-assembly furniture as well.

Perhaps Gillis was named Employee of the Month for this innovation—I am using his first name here since everyone in the company is on a first-name basis. If not, then he certainly deserved the title in 1979, when he sketched a bookcase on a napkin because his colleague, Billy Liljedahl, really wanted one that would be good for books. There it was: the Billy bookcase.

Whatever the reason, it became a bestseller. "The Billy made it possible for everyone to afford their own library," said Lundgren, but was it really the most pressing concern for everyone to finally be able to shelve all their books? Design theorists also tried their hand at analysis, speculating that it was because communities in the 1970s were questioning the traditional nuclear family with its values and furniture, such as wall units and heirlooms. Or maybe it was simply because it fit so well in shared apartments, took up little space, and was also inexpensive. When it disappeared from the catalog in 1990, people protested; in the Stockholm store, customers wore T-shirts that read "Hands off our Billy." Ikea celebrated its return with an ad: "You insulted us. You flattered us. You bribed us. You did it. Billy is back."

Gillis Lundgren | 1978

Billy

It is said that every five seconds, a Billy bookcase is bought somewhere in the world. Ikea has a certain penchant for superlatives. The Scandinavian company maintains that one in ten Europeans is conceived in its beds, and even economic experts can't help but acknowledge its greatness: In 2009, Bloomberg launched a Billy Bookcase Index that, like the Big Mac Index, uses prices in different countries as a guide to the purchasing power of various currencies.

It survived a toxicity scandal in 1992 (*Stern* magazine: "Krank durch Billy"—meaning "Sick by Billy"), artistic sawed-up hacks in 1999 (by artist Rafael Horzon in Berlin), and when Harald Schmidt had 50 bookcases fall over like dominoes in 2009. Not to mention the thousands of men who had problems putting it together.

46

FAILURE OR NOT?
Design fans gasp, so do practitioners. But for completely different reasons.

Philippe Starck | 1990

Juicy Salif

The world is still scandalized over Prince Harry and Meghan. The ungrateful scion of Windsor hightailed it to California—an understandable decision if only for the weather, but there's more to it than that. The three children of his brother William have demoted him to sixth in line for the throne. He's not allowed to take any old job and try to find his own niche. Nor could he be expected to do well in his homeland, caught up in a storm of publicity and under the supervision of his grandmother. If, against all the odds, he managed to outlive all five family members ahead of him in the royal succession, he would be relegated to discharging his duties as an auxiliary king. He's at the height of his powers, all juiced up and ready to go, but with no outlet for his energy. Juice—that's a nice tie-in, but the real crossover between him and Alessi's citrus squeezer is their tragic parallel fates. Although there have been no empirical studies, there's plenty of anecdotal evidence that the Juicy Salif has failed to live up to its name. I'd go so far as to say that most exemplars of Philippe Starck's design piece have never seen the inside of a lemon—which is no loss to the lemon or to the squeezer's owner. Using it to actually extract juice is difficult if not impossible—and, above all, sticky. The tenth anniversary edition from the year 2000 even came with a warning that it should never be used as a juicer. The paint—sorry, the brilliant plating—would quickly be eroded. Author Umberto Eco accused Starck of creating a work of art only as a conversation piece.

But the truth is much more mundane. As Starck sat in an Italian restaurant squeezing a lemon wedge over his calamari, he thought about the noble squid from which his dish originated and hastily scribbled preliminary sketches of the Juicy Salif on his napkin. Alberto Alessi, architect and president of the Alessi design brand, called it "a big joke ... one of the most amusing projects I have done in my career!" And one of his favorites. Juicy Salif adorns the shelves of many a beautiful home, doing what it clearly does best: fare bella figura, cutting a fine figure. And that's good enough for the people of gorgeous, design-oriented Italy, a country where lemons abound. Just don't let them anywhere near Alessi's designer squeezer. Is it possible that Harry and Meghan also have a Juicy Salif on their kitchen counter? That would be an ironic confirmation of their common destiny.

47

For almost 50 years, Ulm artist Peter Dreher had painted the same motif every day: a drinking glass. Always in the same place on a table in his studio. It was a lifelong attempt to find an answer to an important question: Is painting only as important as the subject, and what in fact defines it? The constant repetition made the subject meaningless, but what remained were order, brushstrokes, colors. All of which depended on the light and the weather that day. Which were never the same. Anselm Kiefer, who is much better known, once said that Dreher had been his most important teacher. Dreher died in 2020. The answer to his question, if he ever found it in the glass, he took with him to the grave.

That's how it goes sometimes: A question runs through our lives, a theme, a task. Sometimes we find it ourselves, sometimes others place it in our hands. Chance. Or family. Your mother, for instance. Such was the case with Danish designer Poul Henningsen. In the early 1920s, his mother, Agnes, complained to him about the newfangled incandescent light bulbs that were beginning to replace candles and gas lighting. Agnes thought that these things were blinding, and of course she was right. What she certainly couldn't have imagined was that her son, Poul, came to regard her criticism as his life's work. As far as incandescent light bulbs were concerned, he himself soon proved to be downright averse to light. He hated them, called them "muffin," and did everything he could to try to alleviate his mother's annoyance.

Poul Henningsen | 1958

Artichoke

Initially, Henningsen had designed this lamp for a Copenhagen restaurant: a true modern chandelier with 72 copper plates and 12 light bulbs.

Henningsen's first attempts to control light resulted in lamps for which his hometown of Copenhagen really should have awarded him a medal. The sea of lights at the Tivoli amusement park would have been a fantastic target for bombers during the war if he hadn't invented an ingenious blackout lighting system that made the Tivoli disappear as if under a cloak of invisibility. Thanks to his ingenuity, residents of Copenhagen were able to continue spinning on the carousels and soaring high through the air on the Ferris wheel until midnight without a care in the world. Afterwards, he experimented with shades and bodies of glass, which he placed on top of each other until the light source itself was no longer visible, only the delicate glow reflected by the shades and filtered through the bodies.

With the PH 5 lamp, Henningsen created a bestseller that has since hung in half of all Danish households, according to expert estimates. But the master went one better—four, to be precise. The Septima had seven copper shades and, after its production was discontinued, became the basis for a true masterpiece: the pine cone. Doesn't ring a bell? No surprise, because it became known as the artichoke. Henningsen had been commissioned to design beautiful statement lighting for the chic Langelinie Pavillonen restaurant in Copenhagen—and decided not to reinvent the wheel. Based on the Septima, he created an 80-centimeter pendant light with 72 copper plates that concealed 12 light bulbs. The copper warmed the cold light, and the overlapping plates eliminated all the glare. After 100 lamp designs, he had finally defeated the incandescent light bulb, tamed it, and brought it under control.

In the 1960s, the artichokes made of copper plates became bestsellers, and after Henningsen's death, the manufacturer also introduced pieces in stainless steel and white. Poor Poul would have turned over in his grave. Unfortunately, he was in good company. The legacy of his colleague, Arne Jacobsen, was posthumously desecrated as well. After Jacobsen passed away, the manufacturer changed the design of his ant chair, which originally had only three legs, to four for the sake of stability. When you see the Artichoke lamp in copper, you know immediately that people with style live here. And presumably with money.

Looks like a sculpture, but the Artichoke lamp is absolutely functional. One can use it as a central light source or hang it in a row. It is a work of art in any case.

Every now and again, you read about unbelievable treasures that people turn up while strolling through a flea market. Paintings by great masters that lay forgotten in crates. Vases that, when appraised, turn out to be originals from the distant past and not cheap Chinese knock-offs. And so we envy the young man who bought a kind of display panel for a few cents in a London junk shop in 2009, which was later discovered to be part of Hall 9000, the talking computer from Stanley Kubrick's 1968 film masterpiece: *2001: A Space Odyssey*. A couple of years later, the lucky buyer sold it for 20,000 euros. All the more remarkable, since Kubrick had ordered all the props from his film to be destroyed a couple of years later at MGM Studios in Borehamwood, afraid that the items could end up in some second-rate science fiction movie.

Some of the pieces were, however, ordinary objects of everyday life whose futuristic design made them perfect for the film. Before filming began, Kubrick was said to have asked a number of prominent furniture manufacturers to imagine what their most modern items would look like in a couple of decades. A few designers didn't even have to task their imaginations, but were able to deliver real-life pieces of furniture right to the set. Olivier Mourgue's Djinn Chair, which was quite new at the time, and its contemporary, the Action Office Desk by George Nelson, landed on the cast list. They were joined by a table, which had reached the ripe old age of eleven years, by the time filming began: Eero Saarinen's Tulip Table from 1957.

Eero Saarinen | 1957
Tulip Table

The Finnish designer, who ran an architecture company in Michigan, had not been thinking of the future when he designed the iconic piece of furniture. He'd been focusing entirely on the present, as he was constantly complaining about the lack of legroom whenever he sat down to dinner. He hated what he described as a "leg ghetto," that "ugly, confusing, unruly world" beneath tables and chairs. This naturally arose from the fact that the furniture itself placed four legs into competition with each other. For five years, he tirelessly sketched ideas, built models, wracked his brains, and invited family and friends to test various seats in his home in Bloomfield Hills, Michigan. In the end, the Tulip Table and its chairs, known as the Pedestal Collection, met Saarinen's exacting standards.

Incidentally, the first Tulip Chairs succumbed to a deadly childhood disease in 1956. Made entirely of a single piece of fiberglass-reinforced plastic, they initially kept breaking. Only when Rilsan-coated aluminum strengthened their base, and the fiberglass-reinforced shell was placed in top, did the chair become strong enough to bear weight. And it even rose to the status of film star: It stood on the bridge of the Enterprise in the TV series *Star Trek*, albeit in slightly modified form. After the series was cancelled, the most of the pieces on the set ended up in the trash. Was the Tulip Chair rescued by a light-fingered passer-by? A clever thief? Someone must have gotten their hands on one of these chairs, because it resurfaced at an auction in Hollywood years later. And went for 18,000 US dollars. The chair is now available for sale in any shop, radiant in its magnificence and beauty. The wonderful Tulip Table can be purchased as well, in black, white, or with a marble top. If you happen to discover it at a flea market, be warned: The Tulip Table has been copied more times than any other design.

48

The Tulip table and chairs are so simple because Eero Saarinen found that too many legs were annoying.

If you haven't written an old-fashioned letter in a while, you might want to change that on January 23. That is when National Handwriting Day is celebrated every year—news that probably mainly makes its rounds in an e-mail, however. John Hancock was born on this day in 1737, and he later famously signed the United States Declaration of Independence using a quill pen. Even today, nearly 300 years later, people in the United States still request, "Please put your John Hancock here!" when it comes to signing contracts. That doesn't change the fact that most writing implements have been considered hopelessly outdated ever since keyboards took over our desks.

In 2014, this rivalry even stepped into the realm of science as part of a psychological study conducted by researchers at Princeton University and the University of California, Los Angeles, in which laptops came off badly. The researchers concluded that students who take notes longhand retain the subject matter better than those who took notes on laptops. "The pen is mightier than the keyboard," was the title of the article about the study. After all, twelve brain areas are active when using a pen, plus more than 30 muscles and 17 joints. Although handwriting may be regarded as somewhat old fashioned in our lives today, there is no denying that it is also a matter of tradition. As far back as 5,000 years ago, people in Mesopotamia and Egypt were carving symbols into clay or drawing characters on papyrus using feathers or reeds.

Gerd A. Müller | 1966

Lamy 2000

And yes, we are keeping it traditional and sticking with the pen. Especially since we appreciate the design of a keyboard less than that of a ballpoint pen, for instance. Let's consider the Lamy 2000. When it was launched onto the market in 1966, it really shook up the industry. Up to that point, people usually made their status statements with a gold fountain pen, which they liked to attach to their shirt pockets with its decorative clip as a visible showpiece. With its matte plastic and sleek stainless steel clip, the Lamy 2000 made a contemporary statement of its own. It was regarded as a symbol of understatement and modernity. And, incidentally, it symbolized a generational shift at the company itself: Manfred Lamy, son of manufacturer Carl Josef Lamy, loved the reduced design language; he had the company's development center built as a black glass cube suspended from steel cables and pylons. Chichi was really not his thing. Gerd A. Müller, who had previously designed kitchen appliances and razors at Braun, designed the Lamy 2000 as well—you might say that it also bore his signature in every feature.

It still exists to this day. With head held high, it dances across documents—and twelve brain areas, 30 muscles, and 17 joints dance right along with it. This is how thoughts are set in motion. And even between the lines, you can show a great sense of style! That would be difficult with a computer.

49

Still one of the most modern writing instruments today: the Lamy 2000.

Good help is hard to find. This sentiment certainly has the makings for quirky wall decor, and in cheesy movies it could come up in a conversation between two annoyed aristocrats. In reality, however, you would think it would only ever escape the lips of an HR manager over an after-work beer. Nevertheless, it is thanks to this statement, or at least a similar one, that we owe the invention of a product that makes life so much easier for us, especially in large families or when we invite friends over for dinner: the dishwasher. It was invented by a woman who, goodness knows, was not accustomed to dealing with dirty plates and cups because she had servants for that. In any case, it is striking that a certain distance from the work itself was apparently quite conducive to the development of all kinds of household aids. The draining rack for sinks, frozen food, the first hand-held vacuum cleaner, the electric iron—they all sprang from the minds of men who themselves were not suspected of lending a hand in the household; the time was simply not yet ripe enough for women's liberation.

Herbert Johnston | 1927

KitchenAid

In any case, the dishwasher could well have come into being amid some sort of hangover. Josephine Cochrane, a wealthy American socialite, threw one party after another, but she became very annoyed about the collateral damage that ensued afterwards when the dishes were being washed. Her kitchen maids would chip the porcelain or break the occasional glass. Wash the dishes herself? Nope. In 1883, she had a railroad mechanic build the world's first dishwasher based on her design. The first models were monstrosities that found a place in hotels or restaurants at best, but in 1913 a suitable version finally reached private households as well.

The KitchenAid: If you own one, you'll want to keep it forever.

50

On the left, the first type of food processor from 1927. It could mix, but kneading for example was still a long way off.

134   Stand blender

First the big idea, then the small solution—that was also the opinion of Herbert Johnston, who in 1914 watched a baker working huge quantities of dough with just a spoon and a lot of elbow grease. He initially brought a mixer to market that was equipped with a bowl that could easily rival the druid's magic potion cauldron in Asterix. A few years later, he delighted housewives (no, that's not sexism, that's historical reality!) with a prototype designed for family use. He started out by having the wives of his employees test it. "It's the best kitchen aid I've ever had," one of women is said to have exclaimed enthusiastically, and thus world's first kitchen appliance was named KitchenAid. The fine-tuning, so to speak, of the external appearance was the responsibility of a man who presumably knew a lot about femininity and shapes, albeit for other reasons: Egmont H. Arens published *Playboy* for a while, which in its time as a cultural magazine tended to highlight naked facts surrounding the fine arts, and otherwise wrote for *Vanity Fair* in addition to his work as an industrial designer. Arens was the man behind the KitchenAid's famous design in 1937, and that design has changed very little since then, apart from the fact that a few more color options have been added for its metal body from time to time. Famous fans: automobile tycoon Henry Ford, and, by all accounts, half of Hollywood. That's no surprise, since people there like well-made, stirring dramas anyway.

Right: The KitchenAid as we know it today.

Dorothee Becker | 1968
Uten.Silo

There really exists such a thing: a kind of aid organization for people who simply have too much stuff. The staff at the Institute for Challenging Disorganization in Texas don't see themselves as a decluttering company, of course, but are researching the phenomenon of clutter on test subjects of all kinds. What they've already found: Not only do people make clutter, but clutter ends up making people—namely, it affects their psyche. Surprisingly, a cluttered home has a less impressive effect on men than on women. Most females become really dissatisfied when they live in chaos. This is not an assumption, but a veritable research result after various measurements of the cortisol level in saliva.

The question of how to keep things tidy has now become a major interior design issue—one that has penetrated an astonishing number of cluttered corners ever since the Japanese Marie Kondo began showering the world with tips on how to shrink one's household. She herself, at least in terms of money, probably hasn't known where to put it since. But decluttering is only one path to bliss; the second is self-cutting. In other words, not accumulating so much in the first place. It's certainly no coincidence that Tiny Houses are so popular right now. What is celebrated as a brand-new idea for living is actually old hat: as early as 1845, the writer Henry David Thoreau moved into a small log cabin in the woods of Massachusetts and wrote his novel *Walden*, a manifesto for living in self-chosen simplicity.

But even in the Tiny House, or perhaps especially there, self-organization is a real task. Life is just too complex to be stored in three or four labeled boxes, and anyone who has tried it quickly realizes that some things defy cataloging and classification. Pure pigeonholing has its pitfalls. Tiny house owners should definitely take a look back at a practical invention from 1968, the Uten.Silo. Made of one piece, ready to receive, an eternally mute servant that stows everything in its sturdy plastic pockets that urgently needs a place to stay. It was invented by Dorothee Becker from Munich. She actually wanted to delight her children with a pedagogically valuable toy when she cut geometric figures out of a wooden board and placed their counterparts in a pile so that the little ones could use them again. Shape theory, made easy, but Becker's children didn't find the game particularly exciting. The wooden board was probably sitting in a corner when it inspired Becker to create a kind of vertical garden for the excesses of clutter. When an idea turns out to be a coup, it's often said that you were just in the right place at the right time, but here I'll bring another parameter into play: the company of the right person. Becker was married to Ingo Maurer, the inventor of the delightful Lucellino and Zettel'z lamps. A bright mind in every sense of the word, the man knew that a good idea sometimes needs midwifery. He invested a quarter of a million marks in a three-ton metal injection mold that could be used to make his wife's Uten.Silo. It became a hit, Vitra took it under its wing, and a second, smaller version was created, the Uten.Silo II. In the USA it is called "Wall-All", which actually also sounds very nice.

A small problem remains: you have to remember in which of its recesses you have deposited which objects. Where is the car key, where is the ballpoint pen, where are the nail scissors? Playing memory in a different way. Maybe Becker's children would have had fun with it, too.

It's all in the mix: Base below, tabletop above, the rest is left to your own imagination.

Japanese architects and designers are said to have a penchant for minimalism, but this is often surprisingly far removed from the reality of living in Nippon. Which doesn't change the fact that its inhabitants are true masters of reduction, of quiet nuances. This is partly due to the language, which plays with different levels in a virtuoso manner—a single change of ending reveals the hierarchical level of the interlocutor, but it is also possible to make oneself understood without words: Japanese women, for example, are able to express their displeasure to their husbands by rearranging the flowers in the ikebana vase in a certain way. This, in turn, requires men who look very closely and can also discover and interpret small details. In probably most countries, men could use a little coaching here.

The Shuffle Table MH1 by Mia Hamborg would be a good training ground for guys who need to practice the art of interpretation. It consists of several imaginatively shaped parts that can always be put together differently; in terms of material, he is there wonderfully woke, because extremely diverse on the road: beech wood, marble, MDF, everything is there, and the noble gets along here quite without prejudice with the seemingly banal. In short: a wonderful mix. With her colorful little table, the Norwegian furniture designer did not, of course, have in mind that housemates express their moods over it, but she wanted to achieve one thing: that the Shuffle immediately puts a smile on our faces. It does, and not least because it evokes childhood memories of colorful rings stacked on top of each other on a wooden pole. That's exactly what you've been able to do since 1955 with the "Clown" from the Swedish wooden toy company Brio, and it was indeed Hamborg's source of inspiration. We didn't suspect it as children, but the Brio clown wasn't just supposed to be fun, it was supposed to make us more mature: recognizing colors and sequences was on the secret timetable as soon as we picked up the rings, which were also supposed to train the coordination of our eyes and hands. That's just the way it is with educational toys, they never come around the corner without ulterior motives. So it's even nicer that we're now grown up enough to just have fun with the Shuffle.

Mia Hamborg | 2010

Shuffle Table MH1

52

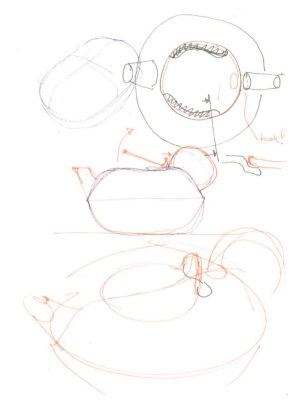

Stefan Diez | 2016

SD

The first time Stefan Diez made an impact was when he was still a boy. At home in Freising, Diez and his father Ernst had used New Year's Eve firecrackers to make an explosive charge, which they decided to set off on a rock while in Italy on vacation. It didn't do the rock any good, but it certainly improved the boy's understanding of the material: rock solid? It's just a word. Under the influence of powerful forces, things can deform and change. A stone that turned into dust was a good example of this.

Since then, Diez has been producing one smash hit after another without any fanfare, but still with an abundance of joy in experimentation: a chair made entirely without screws dubbed Houdini, revolutionary lights that hang from textile strips instead of cables, ultralight chairs. Not to mention a wide range of products, including wood-burning stoves, travel suitcases, and cookware. There's probably nothing Diez hasn't already re-imagined, so it was actually only logical that an exhibition at the 2017 Cologne Furniture Fair showed his entire repertoire. The title: Full House. That says it all, doesn't it?

You never really see Diez without his baseball cap. He's a tinkerer who started out as a carpenter, then wanted to become an architect, and at the last minute turned towards product design. He takes time for his designs; after all, it takes a while until he has gotten to the heart of something so that he can think of it in a way that is both new and somehow always amazingly different. For this reason alone, Diez was just the right man for one of the anniversary sets of dishes from Arita. To mark its 400th anniversary, Japan's porcelain mecca gave itself a gift by asking 16 international designers to help celebrate by creating a tableware design. Diez came up with ideas that almost made Kawazoe Seizan, the local manufacturer, despair at first: None of his 26 tableware pieces had a ring on the base—a feature that every cup and every plate normally has. He had also stipulated that the porcelain should be no thicker than one millimeter. Diez sent plaster prototypes from his Munich studio to the small town of Arita, where it took Kawazoe Seizan a good 18 months to get it right. SD for 2016/Arita porcelain comes in a chaste white and is impressively simple. The set comes across as so delicate and quiet that you simply can't look away. The teapot, which has a lid that stays on when you pour, is absolutely ingenious. It works without a hitch, right down to the last drop. A brilliant idea—and one that surpassed all expectations.

Stefan Diez designing the SD porcelain, a collaboration with Kawazoe Seizan in the Japanese city of Arita.

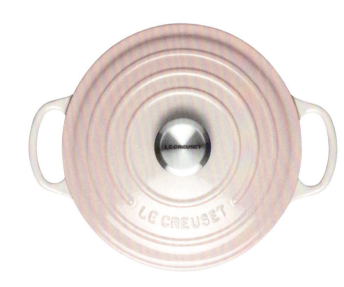

Top left shows the classic Le Creuset roaster in oven red. The classic roaster as well as the La Marmite series with the slightly rounded side walls are available in many colors. One model even shows a lot of heart.

Armand Desaegher and Octave Aubecq | 1925
Le Creuset Cookware

The age of alchemy is usually thought to be long gone. Yet behind the word, which evokes images of mysterious glass vials steaming and bubbling in medieval cellar laboratories, there is one basic question above all: What happens when you combine one material with another? For centuries, people hoped to use alchemy to discover the secret of gold. Seen in this light, Armand Desaegher and Octave Aubecq were plagued by an almost modest ambition. One was a specialist in cast iron, the other worked in enamel, and both decided at a meeting at a Brussels trade fair in 1924 to combine their expertise in both materials and cover cast iron pots with enamel. *Against all odds*, so to speak, because marrying the two materials was considered to be utterly impossible because cast iron expands when heated, while enamel shatters when subjected to heat. The endeavor thus seemed like a physical no-go, but their flirtation with the mere idea promised to be revolutionary. Although cast iron was a hit as a heat conductor, food residue would easily burn onto it, it was difficult to clean, and if you were unlucky, it would start to rust—not exactly the flavor carrier you prefer. Using an enamel coating over the cast iron would solve the problem—and make the kitchen a little more colorful as well.

The two Belgians chose the small town of Fresnoy-le-Grand as the location for their test laboratory. There they spent a year tearing their hair out until they finally successfully achieved the seemingly impossible: A thin wall of cast iron was covered with an enamel coating that could withstand high heat. They named their new company Le Creuset, meaning "the crucible." The first specimens were a bright orange-red, which looked as if the iron was still glowing.

It became a smash hit—and still is. Marilyn Monroe supposedly owned the complete range, and Madonna (she cooks?) and George Clooney also swear by these hot products from France. Meanwhile, the time of challenges is far from over—it's just that we now face new ones. Such as the fact that not everyone manages to pronounce the brand correctly. A cute YouTube video shows how famous American TV chef Vivian Howard keeps trying to pronounce the brand name correctly. Everyone, repeat after me: luh-croo-ZAY. See, that's not so hard!

In general, pieces of furniture stand around rather indifferently. They do nothing. Still, don't let that peaceful image fool you; there's a war raging in the industry. It's about culture, but because culture is something that we all hold dear, it's obviously also about money. Money is quickly earned with design pieces, and that is why the business of counterfeits and knock-offs is flourishing. Icons in particular have to live with the fact that they are likely to encounter any number of look-alikes on the market. Needless to say, the manufacturers of these pieces do not accept this without complaint. For instance, every year Thonet hires Stephan von Petersdorff-Campen, a lawyer from Düsseldorf specializing in copyright law, to track down knock-offs. He does so by scouring the international furniture trade show in Cologne in search of replicas of Thonet classics that are far too similar to the originals. In 2015, a Chinese manufacturer unceremoniously locked him in the office of his trade show booth when the lawyer attempted to remove one of the exhibited chairs from the display.

In the case of Bauhaus furniture, there are now probably far more fakes than originals in circulation—much to the chagrin of the manufacturers. The classics are expensive collector's items. If you own an original, you are always on the right track or have a viable investment—depending on whether it's a couch, a chair, or a table. The price of furniture from this period in particular is the subject of frequent debate. Although Bauhaus designers explicitly set out to make living affordable for everyone, unfortunately their good intentions were carried to the grave with them. Their legacy, which they presumably never wanted, was hefty licensing fees that drove up prices. With Bauhaus, there's another rather nasty issue on the front line: Sometimes it's no longer clear who actually had which brilliant idea first. Mart Stam and Marcel Breuer, for example, both worked with bold tubular steel frames. Back in 1932, a court had to clarify the copyright and awarded Stam the rights to the "cubic chair without back legs" (▶ p. 224). Marcel Breuer was furious about the decision. In later years, he sold the rights to many of his designs to the Italian company Gavina. The B3 Club chair, which was better known as the Wassily Chair from the 1960s onwards, had three different versions—rigid, flexible, and foldable—and Breuer sold each version to a different manufacturer. There was a lot of trouble about one of his works in particular: his small minimalist side table made of tubular steel and a laminate top. Tecta, a company in Lauenförde that had acquired the license directly from Breuer's widow, once produced it as the B 9 stool. Knoll International, which bought all the licenses from Gavina, has it in its lineup as the Laccio table. To further complicate matters, at some point a company in Stendal also entered the scene with a much cheaper copy. The confusion was resolved in 2002: The table was officially promoted from a piece of furniture to a work of art, and the company with the oldest rights was selected—a victory for Knoll International. Tecta was forced to destroy its entire inventory of B 9 stools. Nevertheless, a few managed to escape the decree: In Dessau, you can still sit on a B 9 stool today. In the Bauhaus cafeteria, of all places.

Marcel Breuer | 1925

Laccio

The Flower Pot lamp likes to make the splash of color in the apartment. In matte white, on the other hand, it looks very elegant.

Verner Panton | 1968

FlowerPot

Even style has its intergenerational conflicts, young brutes who leap onto the stage, shove the veteran company aside, and do their best to stir things up. They bide their time for a while, patiently and politely watching the drama being played out, until they decide to hijack the program and shine a spotlight on their own revolutionary ideas. It happens in the best of style families, even those where harmony has appeared to reign, where the community has agreed on natural materials, a high level of craftsmanship, subtle colors, and lots of black and white as the ingredients that make for a cozy interior. Arne Jacobsen, Hans J. Wegner, Finn Juhl, Børge Mogensen, and many others were the original founders of Danish classic, the Nordic mid-century modern, and even today these northern lights remain surprisingly true to their values, which we now know as the Scandinavian style.

In his day, Verner Panton wanted to learn from the best and became an assistant to a star architect, Arne Jacobsen. He probably helped him with his legendary "ant," a chair that originally stood on three legs. Secretly, however, his head was filled with very different, much more colorful ideas. As early as the beginning of the 1950s, he was already relying less on nature and more on a new material, plastic. Instead of simple elegance, he strove for sensational effects. His engagement with color psychology while studying at the Danish Academy of Fine Arts in Copenhagen was not for nothing. By 1952, he had learned all he could from Jacobsen, so he packed his bags and embarked on a three-year sabbatical, crisscrossing Europe in his VW bus. When he finally resurfaced, he designed chairs and a demountable house that could also be repurposed as a garage. In 1960, he achieved his first masterpiece in plastic with the iconic Panton Chair, a cantilever chair cast in a single piece that went into series production in 1967 under the Vitra brand. The time was ripe for Panton and his colorful ideas that also signaled a break with traditions. Student protests against the Vietnam War, the establishment, and the stuffiness of tradition fueled a social upheaval. Panton shared the young people's psychedelic ideas. His dreams were multicolored and loud. Scott McKenzie was singing the hippy anthem of the time, "If you're going to San Francisco, be sure to wear some flowers in your hair." We don't know whether Panton ever actually put a flower behind his ear during those wild days, but his solidarity with the spirit of the new generation bore remarkable fruit. He created his famous Flowerpot lamp—basically, two semi-spheres placed one on top of the other—in his own design studio in 1967. It was a brash statement that's available today in all the colors of the rainbow. The lamp actually became a symbol of its day, although I for one can't see what it has to do with a flower pot. But it's beautiful, and extremely compatible, fitting best in interiors furnished with pieces by Jacobsen, Wegner, Juhl, etc. On the one hand, it's clearly a child of its time. On the other hand, it's marvelously timeless. That's not an easy feat to pull off.

They keep telling us that sitting is the new smoking. So maybe we have turned sedentariness into an art form, but we still need a soft place to park our bottoms. Even people in the Stone Age must have preferred a seat on steppe grass to one on cave rocks. The fact is, sometime in the Middle Ages our lives became much more cushy, starting with simple straw mats that were later covered in beautiful cloth—but that was already the Renaissance. During the Baroque period, everything became slightly exaggerated, not just on the gaudiness scale but also in terms of upholstery. For those with lots of money, it was a way of showing that they were above it all, and particularly above the rest of humanity. Aristocrats, kings, everyone who belonged to the better society pampered themselves by upholstering their armchairs, sofas, and beds with palm fibers and horsehair, and the most genteel among them could even brag about their extreme sensitivity—like the princess and the pea. Several centuries went by until finally, in 1937, an aspiring chemist named Otto Bayer mixed together a few polyester derivatives—the exact names escape me—in a trash can and got a reaction. Bayer had accidentally invented plastic foam.

Annie Hiéronimus | 1980

Plumy

We had to wait a while longer for polyurethane—an insulating material that could be softer or harder, flexible or rigid—to make our everyday lives softer. After the Second World War, people were still trying to sit up straight on sofas. Upholstered furniture wasn't something you sank into but something that helped you maintain an upright posture. Then in the early 1970s, young people sprawled on mattresses on the floors of tea rooms and communes, and in the 1980s, the comfort trend finally reached the suburban living room. It was early in this laid-back decade—exactly the right moment in time—that Parisian designer Annie Hiéronimus, who had been working at Ligne Roset since 1976, invented Plumy: the plump and cuddly sofa with a foam core and goose feather-filled seat and backrest cushions that you could fold down and stretch out on. After taking a creative break, Plumy suddenly reappeared in 2016, ready for whatever came its way. Plumy is like sitting on a cloud that makes you forget all your troubles, a partner you can lean on and who will catch you when you fall. In the Baroque age, it would have been the rulers' choice for a throne. And somehow I'm sure that if the princess could have had Plumy, she wouldn't have noticed the pea.

57

Plumy: the epitome of exceptional seating comfort and French savoir-faire.

Massimo Vignelli | 1966

Stendig

The original meanings of words are sometimes forgotten. Some 200 years ago, for example, feminism was understood to mean the undesirable growth of breasts in men and only came to be used in an equal rights context around 1900. At the end of the 19th century, a robot was still a sort of slave serving noble lords and only took on the meaning of a mechanical man when Karel Capek introduced it in his drama *R.U.R.* in 1920. The word "newspaper" was originally meant to highlight the news and not the paper on which it was printed. And the only purpose of the first calendar was to serve Mammon. It was a registry of debts in which ancient Roman moneylenders kept track of the days on which interest came due.

Some people today could still benefit from such careful attention to due dates, but I hope most of them are mainly using their own calendars as a place to enter birthdays, weddings, meals with friends, and visits to the zoo or theater. If you still have a foot in the analog world, you probably have one hanging on your wall. Landscapes, sports, and animal motifs are extremely popular, and then there are works of the great masters. Looked at in this way, it's puzzling that the design-obsessed MoMA in New York was so taken with this particular calendar that they immediately added it to their permanent collection. Its creator, Massimo

58

Vignelli, literally turned the calendar back into a set of numbers. All right, he kindly added the few letters necessary for identifying the days of the week. It's uncannily simple, altogether minimalistic, with colors that tend toward the austere—nothing but alternating black and white. The concept is actually so simple that in its own description, the company could think of nothing more distinctive to say about it than: "Sheets are detachable, designed to be removed at the end of each month." The height of understatement. But it's also sure to appear in some living rooms. In terms of format, Vignelli's monster suffers from megalomania. Measuring 3 feet by 4 feet, it definitely makes a statement, but not a bad one. Attaching any picture or quotation to the monthly jumble of dates could also be interpreted as adding flourishes and unnecessary decorations, which is totally out of line with Vignelli's design requirements. And if we look at it philosophically, the months have no pictures because it's up to us to supply them with pictures.

Vignelli was also a minimalist when it came to fonts. In the new computer age, as he used to complain, there are "thousands of fonts. We just need some basic fonts, the rest can be thrown away!" He generally settled on Helvetica for his calendar, but also for other designs. New York's subway signs, its subway map, Bloomingdale's brown shopping bags—all by Vignelli. In 1981 Michael Bierut, an employee at his firm, described the city as "a permanent Vignelli exhibition." Vignelli was also responsible for the American Airlines logo. If it had been left up to the master, he would have practiced the art of omission and done away with the eagle. Years later he was still grumbling about how it was forced on him by the client.

As for the calendar, the Milan-born artist actually returned it to its own roots. His invention was also merely a matter of numbers—and of money, of course. Every year, Vignelli's masterpiece still sells out immediately.

„We prefer designs that are visually strong, intellectual, elegant and above all timeless," explained Massimo Vignelli, designer of the Stendig calendar.

Eileen Gray | 1927
Tube Light

Many designers became architects as a secondary or even primary profession, which presumably has to do with the passion for aesthetics with which they are afflicted or perhaps blessed. Maybe they find bad style even more painful than do other people. In any case, they like to design everything all around them. However, this near-messianic dedication completely backfired on Le Corbusier. He admired House E-1027, designed by Eileen Gray and where she lived with her partner, the architect Jean Badovici, 15 years her junior, near Monaco on the Côte d'Azur. Le Corbusier painted enormous colorful murals on the walls. Badovici had no objection, but Eileen Gray, who was out of the house at the time, was not happy. It ended a long friendship between the Frenchman and the Irish-born designer. And it prompted Gray to move out of her house and refuse to ever enter it again.

Nevertheless, she was stuck with Le Corbusier. In some respects, he remained part of her most important designs. Although Gray's genius shines through the 1927 Tube Light, her friendship with the Bauhaus master did indeed lend her style a definite functional quality. While the painted furniture she created from 1910 onward show clear hints of Art Deco style, the designs she developed while exchanging ideas with the Bauhaus movement are much clearer and more functional. A long tube, an equally long lightbulb, a round metal base. That's all there is to the Tube Light. But for all its technical clarity, the lamp glows with a wonderful warmth. It is sometimes described as the precursor to the fluorescent tube light, which entered world history in 1936, and Gray could arguably be celebrated as a visionary after the fact. However, this would place her iconic light in the shadows.

Indeed, Gray came up with what may well be her most famous design the same year as the Tube Light: the E 1027 side table made from steel tubes and glass. It does, in fact, bear the same name as her house on the French Riviera, the reason for which is not quite as functional. E 1027 is an expression of Gray's love for her dubious life partner Jean Badovici. E stands for Eileen, the tenth letter of the alphabet is J, for Jean, 2 represents the B in Badovici, the 7 is the G in the designer's last name.

By the way, House E 1027 did not do particularly well after being splattered with colorful paint. It fell into ruin over the course of time, and, in the 1990s, uninvited guests frequently went on rampages in its empty rooms. But then, in 2008, the house was finally renovated and declared a French National Cultural Monument. It reopened in 2021 as a museum, filled with Gray's furniture designs. Corbusier's murals were removed. Perhaps Madame Gray got her own back in the afterlife.

Subtly elegant and extremely progressive: With her Tube Light, Eileen Gray was way ahead of her time, as the fluorescent tube was actually first introduced a decade later.

Patricia Urquiola | 2006

Antibodi

A cookie-cutter product won't win you any prizes, and it certainly won't make you famous. As a product designer, this puts you in a tricky situation, or—if you want to remain in the profession—you may find yourself on the fence. If you simply focus on practical value when designing, the result threatens to slide into blandness. If you are too fussy, the result may be art, but the furniture may not be suitable for everyday use. In fact, the difference between design and art often lies in practicality. Good design should not look like a home improvement store, but it shouldn't resemble something out of a museum either. And it is only the marriage of the two that achieves a higher level. "A fashion that does not reach the streets is not a fashion," Coco Chanel famously concluded of haute couture. "Luxury must be comfortable, otherwise it is not luxury." That's something the big names in the interior design industry would do well to remember. You have to be able to sit on chairs, spread out all kinds of things on tables, rest comfortably on beds—but all of that should preferably be strikingly beautiful.

In many pieces, Spanish designer Patricia Urquiola has demonstrated a clear sense of comfort, but with the lounge chair, for which in 2006 she was marveled at, loved, and admired, she succeeded above all in creating a piece of art. Designed for the label Moroso, Antibodi is an eye-catcher that will earn you envious glances in your own home and is sure to provoke the curious question: "Can I try it out?" A word of warning, however: You may not easily be able to persuade your visitors to get up again because they find your furniture so comfortable.

Everyone knows that a bed of roses is not particularly comfortable, even meadows of flowers can prick, and sometimes replicas of nature share the same characteristics: The artfully folded flower appliqués made of felt, wool, and leather are quite

Unusual shapes for a piece of seating furniture: a creation of triangular petals sewn together to create generous geometries.

striking after all, and are perceived as such when you touch them. But perhaps it would be better not to touch the lounge chair after all, because the wit is all in the surface. And as soon as somebody sprawls across it, that wit is obscured. Urquiola has made her mark with this design and demonstrated the artistic realms in which she knows how to move. "Furniture is a tool for living, for life, and it has to be fun," is the philosophy of the woman who never really wanted to be a designer because she thought they only made chairs. Antibodi is definitely fun. For the eyes if nothing else.

Left: If the petals are directed upward, the result is a slightly eccentric, decorative shape—if they are curved downward, the result is a deliberately austere look.

This page: Patricia Urquiola never really wanted to be a designer. Good thing she changed her mind!

The son of a Japanese poet and an American writer created a truly sculptural coffee table.

160   Coffee table

Isamu Noguchi | 1947
Coffee Table

There are some accessories that people would kill for—Hermés scarves, Louis Vuitton handbags, Prada sunglasses, the little black dress by Chanel. And who knows, maybe the abundant availability of counterfeits of these coveted objects deters some people from committing robbery, homicide, or at the very least, petty larceny. But that would be the only good thing to come out of these ignoble copies of noble brands. But enough shaming and blaming, the furniture world is just as rife with barbaric fakery. Almost all classics have to put up with dozens of alter egos. Anything that succeeds will be shamelessly copied. The knockoff has been punished from the very beginning, but wasn't lambasted with an anti-prize until 1977. Each year, the most flagrant imitations are chosen to receive the "Plagiarius" award, which takes the form of a black dwarf with a golden nose. Naturally, the recipients don't show up in person to accept their awards, the journey would be too far—many would have to come from China. But these counterfeits do have their own exhibition. The Museum Plagiarius in Solingen, Germany, houses a collection of over 350 examples of identity theft.

For the designers who have poured their hearts, souls, and money into a brilliant idea, it must be devastating to find out that someone else is making a bundle at their expense. Fortunately, this experience failed to undermine the half-Japanese designer and sculptor Isamu Noguchi. He designed a coffee table with a three-legged rosewood base in 1939 for A. Conger Goodyear, who was then director of the New York Museum of Modern Art. Not long afterwards, his British colleague T. H. Robsjohn-Gibbings asked him to design a desk for his office. Noguchi was extremely busy at the time and hastily sent him the plastic model of his design for Goodyear. He never received a response—but he did run into serious trouble.

The attack on Pearl Harbor caused difficulties for the Japanese community in the United States. Many of them were put in internment camps. Noguchi would have been spared this ordeal, but he moved into the Relocation Center in Poston, Arizona, of his own free will as an act of solidarity. He wanted to teach classes in design and handicrafts to make this period of suffering more bearable for his fellow countrymen, and he even designed pools and gardens for the camps. None of them were ever built and Noguchi never received the promised materials for his classes. The camp became his prison, as well.

One day he was looking through a magazine and saw an ad for a table exactly like the model he had sent to Robsjohn-Gibbings. His colleague had produced it behind his back and made a huge profit. Although Noguchi was never compensated, he did experience some satisfaction. He refined his original model and came up with a masterpiece, the famous coffee table: two organically curved pieces of wood and a drop-shaped glass sheet. "The best design I ever made," Noguchi later said. The world agreed. And please note: The truth will out, works of plagiarism eventually fade into obscurity. Golden-nosed dwarves should be ashamed of themselves.

FAILURE OR NOT? Not a piece of cake to manufacture—and at times a bit slow to sell, too.

162 Toy

Charles and Ray Eames | 1945
Elephant

The saying that opposites attract obviously originated with a very unreliable source. Research shows that the contrary is true. We most easily fall in love with the people who are closest to us in all respects. Eighty percent of couples in rural areas lived within a 20-kilometer radius of each other when they were single, and in cities this figure is as high as 90 percent. Many couples also come from the same social class. Algorithms on dating websites are designed to comb through profiles for similarities and proximity when calculating matches, because the closer the match, the deeper the feelings. Attraction is often a matter of loving your neighbor.

When Charles Eames and Ray Kaiser fell in love, they were even working on the same project. She was a student assistant for one of his exhibitions that he was supervising as a director at the Cranbrook Academy of Art. At some point, he scribbled a disarmingly romantic marriage proposal on the Academy's letterhead, providing her with the information that he was almost 34, newly single, completely broke, might never be able to support her, but was relatively anxious to get married. Ray said yes and the rest is history.

Charles and Ray Eames lived, designed, and dreamed together, gave the world unforgettable beauty—and drew elephants. Pachyderms might seem a little incongruous at this point, but they were a fact. This was one more area in which the couple was especially united. They loved elephants, they kept stacks of elephant photos, and they were passionate about painting them. At the time, Charles was experimenting with molding plywood, which he had used in the Second World War to make leg braces and stretchers for soldiers. After the war, he employed the leftovers to make two elephants that served as seats. It was just for fun, a sort of test balloon, but it extended the couple's target group for molded plywood furniture that they were currently working on to include children. However, it turned out that the wooden elephants were too unwieldy and complicated to manufacture so, unfortunately, they ended up with Lucia Eames, Charles' 14-year-old daughter, and later in a museum. It wasn't until the celebration of Charles Eames' 100th birthday in 2007 that Vitra issued a limited cherry wood edition for adults and a plastic version for children. Although it was more of a posthumous birthday present than a bestseller, it was still beautiful and a symbol of the playfulness shared by one of the greatest designer couples of all time.

Also available one size smaller and simply enchanting as a colorful herd: the Eames Elephant made of plastic.

The Eames Elephant is an expression of pure creative joy. Unfortunately, production was somewhat cumbersome at the time. Today, it is made by Vitra from fine cherry wood.

Sometimes I wish the Japanese concept of wabi sabi would have a greater influence on our Western perceptions. Blemishes, scratches, and imperfections are recognized only as mere insignia of maturity and valued as true signs of nobility. Wabi sabi gives aging objects the immediate distinction of being especially valuable. Whimsical ceramic pieces in particular fetch high prices in Japan. We in the West also delight in this philosophy, we rave about worn surfaces and find moving words to describe pieces that have survived at least one but usually multiple lifetimes. Too bad we don't apply the same concept to creases, crow's feet, and wrinkled skin.

But before we get caught up in a tirade against age discrimination, let's quickly shift back to the subject of stylish Japan. There, too, wabi sabi is associated with a fundamental condition, the fact that we only admire things that have aged gracefully, which normally only applies to natural materials. Wooden bowls, ceramic pots, metal spoons, and similar objects can look forward an illustrious future—not as part of a momentary trend but as a reflection of a certain attitude toward life.

Something similar can be said of the tea ceremony. Long ago, it served as a stage for honoring the most expensive showpieces and social hierarchies—until tea master Sen no Rikyu replaced its conceit with austere simplicity. He believed that making tea was merely a matter of boiling water, preparing the tea, and drinking it. In today's traditional tea ceremonies, masters still present guests with old, handmade ceramic cups, which they're expected to hold reverently in their hands while thoroughly examining and admiring their irregularities before the foamy green tea is poured. To ensure that their teacups would be as simple and unassuming as possible, the masters often made their own pottery, or else they ordered vessels from the local prefectures that were known for their porcelain art. Masahiro Mori came from just such a region, the Saga prefecture, where he followed in the footsteps of many of his compatriots and studied ceramics and ceramic design. He ultimately worked for the Hakusan Porcelain Company in Nagasaki, creating contemporary, everyday tableware. Hakusan must have been congratulating itself for decades afterwards for having embraced this young man whose incredibly simple designs were simply ingenious. In 1958, Mori designed an unprepossessing vessel for soy sauce, the G-Type Pitcher, that became a bestseller, a top export, and continues to be the star of the collection today. It even graces the cover of the exhibition catalog of the National Museum of Modern Art in Tokyo. Its price has since risen from 130 yen, which is barely one euro, to around 25 euros, but as a genuine design piece, the pitcher is still a bargain. And if soy sauce isn't your thing, this humble object will also tolerate oil and vinegar, and even gravy in an emergency. It's a genuine global player.

Masahiro Mori | 1958

G-type

63

Masahiro Mori: „My pleasure as a designer is to conceive forms for everyday use so that many people can appreciate and enjoy it."

Today, the only probably unused Vipp pedal bin is in the Museum of Modern Art in New York, right next to contemporary and modern art. A real accolade for a garbage bin!

It's more likely to crash in a plane or be born with six toes than to win the lottery, yet millions of people dream of millions that probably won't make them happy after all: In 1956, a man in his mid-forties named Walter Knoblauch hit the first jackpot in the history of the German lottery, won it again two years later, but squandered the money in no time at all and ended up impoverished in a homeless shelter in 1995. A young man from Remels, who won one and a half million marks in 1974, fared little better. He relied on false friends and advisors who talked him into highly speculative investments, and today has to live on a rather meager pension.

Holger Nielsen | 1939

Vipp

There are a disappointingly large number of such examples, which is why the Dane Holger Nielsen deserves a symbolic pat on the back: although he didn't win any money in 1931, he did win a car in the Danish lottery. Unfortunately, he didn't get a driver's license to go with it, so Nielsen couldn't do much with the vehicle and traded it in for a metal lathe. A decision that changed everything for Nielsen, who earned his living as a dance instructor in the evenings. When his wife complained in 1939 that she didn't have a decent trash can in her hair salon, Nielsen made her one without further ado that had it all: with an inner bucket for removing and cleaning and a non-slip silicone base. In addition, its flap opened and closed pleasantly quietly and practically via a pedal. But that wasn't all: The bucket was also pretty to look at, as it waited so slim and slender to be filled with everything that the world no longer needed. Had no one thought of it before, or had most designers been too shy to give the waste disposal a nice touch? One thing is certain: For Nielsen, the garbage bin became a goldmine.

His invention found its way into hotels, doctors' offices, gas stations and ferries, and 1200 buckets a year left his workshop. Nielsen probably passed on his sense of practicality to his daughter Jette, but unfortunately neither sketches nor construction plans. Nevertheless, she fought her way through, promoted the family heirloom and even took the bucket on a cart to the Ambiente trade fair in Frankfurt to advertise it. Incidentally, her son Kasper Egelund has since taken over the company together with his wife. Everything for the garbage bin? Not at all: The company has neatly expanded its range. Among other things, a transportable, fully equipped vacation home called Vipp Shelter. There, of course, grandfather's trash can is a permanent fixture. In New York's MoMA and in the Louvre in Paris, too, by the way. But he's not available for dirty things there—just as an example of really good design.

Left page: Vipp Heritage Bin from 2020.

Below: He obviously liked elegantly shaped metal: Vipp company founder Holger Nielsen.

Pedal bin

Once your reputation is ruined, you can live quite freely, and let's be honest: This is as true for a great fame that may have befallen you through no fault of your own. If you are suddenly falsely attributed merit, generosity or a clever idea, you can of course defend yourself vehemently. Or you can just shut up and enjoy the gift of nimbus. It is difficult to understand who kept quiet about the truth back then, when the authorship of the Z.Stuhl chair was clearly assigned to the wrong faction. In 1973, the good piece went into series production at the GDR-owned Petrolchemisches Kombinat Schwedt, and from then on it was considered an East German product. The foreign feathers with which it was adorned in the socialist republic were just too dressy, the temptation too great. Probably, one would not have wanted to expose the truth to one's own people: The design of the Z.Stuhl came from the class enemy, straight from the West. There, where the real jeans were also available, which were considered a capitalist evil in their own country in the 1950s and 1960s, where people swayed to English-language rock music, which in the GDR was at best secretly played in youth rooms and garages. In fact, the Z.Stuhl had been invented by Ernst Moeckl, who had trained at the Ulm College of Design. In the early 1960s, he had opened his own office for industrial design, and the Rollei and Nixdorf companies were among his clients. He came up with the Z, which also became known as the "Squatting Man" or "Kangaroo," in 1968. The chair had moderate success as part of the Horner Collection, but party officials in the GDR, who unlike their ordinary citizens sometimes went on shopping trips to the hated West, were highly interested in it. Its material, pure polyurethane, was cheap and willing; it could be used to press shoe soles, mattresses, varnishes, and apparently even a chair from a single mold.

Ernst Moeckl | 1973

Z.Stuhl

Only the processing technology apparently had its limits. According to research by historian Dr. Sebastian Lang from Chemnitz, the GDR bought the license for the chair without further ado and, with Western help, had a plant built in the East—the Petrolchemische Kombinat Schwedt. This was a splendid technology transfer for which the border proved to be astonishingly permeable in the middle of the Cold War.

In Berlin, the press café in the house of the Berlin Verlag is completely furnished with the East German classic.

65

Due to the use of the same plastic and the manually applied lacquer surface, the Z.Stuhl is sometimes compared with the Panton Chair by Danish designer Verner Panton.

174   Chair

The fancy chair suited the political goal in every respect: "Socialism offers the guarantee that people can arrange their lives with practicality and beauty," the handbook on socialist design stated tritely, but at least it was recognized that, in addition to bread, butter and basic supplies, one also had to offer its citizens something for the eye. In addition, Honecker and his cohorts urgently wanted to boost consumption a bit. The people weren't too keen on new purchases; they were used to grief. Before they had to stand in an endless queue again, they preferred to see to it that the things at home lasted a few more years. One took care of one's belongings and spared them or, best of all, didn't use them at all. Even though our collective Western memories of the GDR tend to cast a socialist veil of gray and think of scary prefabricated buildings, people did have fun with joyful design. What they did have, they showed at the Leipzig spring and fall fairs, pretty furniture programs nestled between modern patterns and colors, or pieces that were not even dissimilar to those in the West - like the Sybille shelving system, which bore astonishing traits of the Swedish String bestseller.

So the Z.Stuhl made it to the East, was adopted and celebrated as what it really wasn't: GDR design. Any resistance from the original family? Not that I know of. Perhaps it was also because the chair could never really score in its own home, the West. It had to fight against strong and, above all, well-known competition, which, unfortunately, was not entirely dissimilar to it: the Panton Chair from 1967.

In the East, on the other hand, the red carpet was virtually rolled out for it. Since 2020, it has been restored at the family-owned company Pestel in Chemnitz. For company CEO Liv Pestel, it was by no means love at first sight; in fact, she had been given an old one by her parents as a child and tended to throw her clothes over it in her teenage bedroom. It was only when, long since grown up, she added three more Z.Stuhl chairs as a trial that she fell in love with the piece and decided on its comeback. By the way, the Z.Stuhl will be 50 years old in the summer of 2023. We would like to extend our warmest congratulations.

On a memorable December evening in 1980, the great designer Ettore Sottsass met with several colleagues, including Matteo Thun, Shiro Kuramata, and Michele de Lucchi, in Sottsass' Milan apartment to stage a sort of backroom revolution and decided to violently overthrow the dictates of form and function that had ruled the design world ever since the Bauhaus movement. From that moment on, the group's work would be unrestricted, vulgar, wild, colorful, and sensual. In the background, Bob Dylan was heard singing "Stuck Inside of Mobile with the Memphis Blues Again" when the record started to skip and "Memphis," "Memphis," Memphis" filled the Milan evening. Rock 'n' roll, blues, and resistance—it all fell into place and the new style had found its name. Cabinets constructed from cubes, spheres, and cylinders, slanting shelves, blue, lavender, and green sofas, chairs that were anything but comfortable, tables covered with graphically patterned plastic laminate, which they had previously held to be the paragon of bad taste. The motto "less is more" was deep-sixed in an ocean of kitsch art and replaced with its total opposite: "Less is a bore." This was the atmosphere in which the great Michele de Lucchi created his Kristall, Polar, and Continental side tables, all using the same colors, materials, and shapes. In 1984, the Flamingo completed the quartet, with a neon yellow tabletop representing a beak, a blue footrest, and a bright green pole extending from a black-and-white support—the kind of thing that automatically makes you wonder if something went wrong during its assembly. It certainly is eye-catching, no doubt about that, more of a manifest than furniture, but that's exactly what it was supposed to be. Memphis shocked the world and continues to fascinate us today. Some people fell madly in love with the style when it first came out. Fashion czar Karl Lagerfeld furnished his entire Monte Carlo apartment with it in the 1980s. Ten years later, he couldn't stand it anymore and auctioned it all off. "Too much of a good thing" can apply to anything, and in the case of Memphis, it's best to take just a small bite.

But the zeitgeist is nefarious and the pendulum inevitably swings back. The efforts of Sottsass, de Lucchi, and all the other Memphis designers to create pure anti-design have backfired and landed them and their works in the design museums of this world.

Michele de Lucchi | 1984

Flamingo

The Flamingo side table: quirky counter-draft to the 1970s high-tech style.

Sometimes you might get the impression that younger people think the topic of sustainability has grown up around the same time as they have, just like the awareness for the responsible use of resources. We somewhat more mature adults admit that: We've been pretty sloppy about it in recent decades. But of course, such considerations are not new; in fact, they have been part of the curriculum of design courses for half a century and hope for the interest of the student body. For Axel Kufus from Berlin, now a design professor, working on the edge of a nature reserve in the 1980s sharpened his eye for wood as a resource.

As a young carpenter, he was allowed to cut only those trees that the forester had marked with a cross during a critical tour of his territory. Since then, Kufus recalls, he has been walking through the forest with different eyes—and has also been more conscious in his choice of materials. A few years later, he was working in a Berlin workshop cooperative. The bread-and-butter job: playing fireman when there was a snag somewhere in the exhibition construction or time was running out. The boys jokingly called themselves Red Adair, after the world's most famous fireman, who specialized in fighting large fires. The job of creating a shelf with lots of storage space as quickly as possible was also one of those jobs where they had to shoot from the hip, so to speak.

Axel Kufus | 1989

In 1987, the city of Berlin drew up a land use plan, and every page of the expert opinions, concerns, and statements required for it had to be laid out copied thousands of times over. However, the cooperative was not designed for mass production, and insane quantities of dowels, which would have been needed for conventional shelving, did not exactly fall from

Shelving system

Minimal construction meets maximum ease of use: with distinguished modesty, the FNP shelf adapts to almost any room situation. Below, its creator Axel Kufus.

the sky either. Kufus fiddled around for a night or two, experimenting with coated plywood from the wagon construction industry and MDF boards, which until then had only been used in industry—and came up with a solution that amazed even himself in its simplicity. His shelving unit required no screws, was simply plugged in, and was up and running within 15 minutes. Kufus had always been convinced that simplicity does not come from reduction, but from concentration. And indeed, the Kufus shelf was a combination of know-how, trial and error, and a lot of philosophy: Even during production, one work step seemed to flow into the next, like almost a choreography developed, and that was important to Kufus. The fact that the shelf could only be assembled in just one way, as a logical continuation of this wonderful flow idea, only made it even more perfect. "Form follows production," Kufus is still pleased to say today.

The shelf was christened after its first purpose: FNP—the shortage for the German name for for land use plan. In fact, it soon expanded its horizons in every conceivable direction, outgrew itself in old Berlin buildings with a room height of 3.50 meters, and at some point made itself thin for CDs. It adapted, always and everywhere. And remained, what an understatement, modestly in the background. A star without airs and graces. His father Axel Kufus, once a design professor at the Bauhaus University in Weimar, now teaches design at the University of the Arts in Berlin. His students can also learn sustainability and resource awareness from him. They'll just have to figure out the flow thing for themselves.

Sometimes also referred to as „Bird" or „Tulip": The stylish armchair FK 6725 was originally manufactured by Kill International in Stuttgart-Fellbach in Germany.

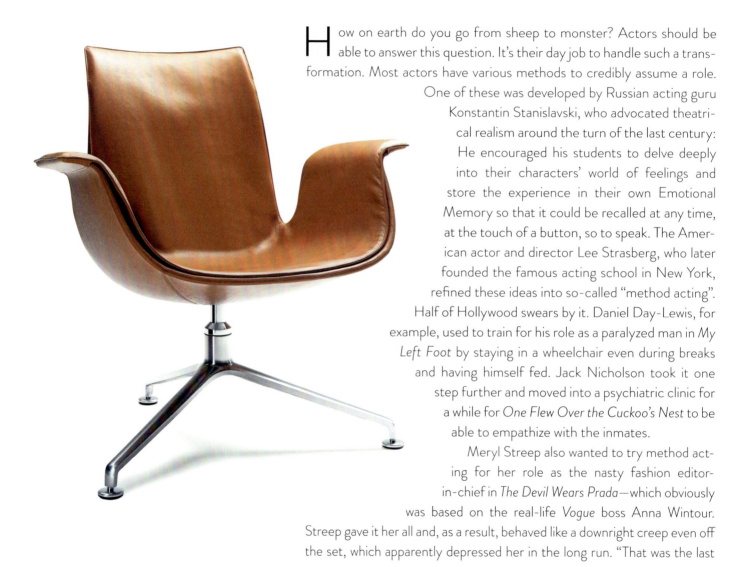

How on earth do you go from sheep to monster? Actors should be able to answer this question. It's their day job to handle such a transformation. Most actors have various methods to credibly assume a role. One of these was developed by Russian acting guru Konstantin Stanislavski, who advocated theatrical realism around the turn of the last century: He encouraged his students to delve deeply into their characters' world of feelings and store the experience in their own Emotional Memory so that it could be recalled at any time, at the touch of a button, so to speak. The American actor and director Lee Strasberg, who later founded the famous acting school in New York, refined these ideas into so-called "method acting". Half of Hollywood swears by it. Daniel Day-Lewis, for example, used to train for his role as a paralyzed man in *My Left Foot* by staying in a wheelchair even during breaks and having himself fed. Jack Nicholson took it one step further and moved into a psychiatric clinic for a while for *One Flew Over the Cuckoo's Nest* to be able to empathize with the inmates.

Meryl Streep also wanted to try method acting for her role as the nasty fashion editor-in-chief in *The Devil Wears Prada*—which obviously was based on the real-life *Vogue* boss Anna Wintour. Streep gave it her all and, as a result, behaved like a downright creep even off the set, which apparently depressed her in the long run. "That was the last

FK 6725

time I tried this Method thing," she said later. She did, however, fill the chair she was given in the movie with grandeur—though this part was also incredibly well cast: The FK 6725 has exactly the urban chic you'd expect from a fashion director. Clean. Glamorous, stylish, and wrapped in fine leather, it was the perfect companion in her daily editorial routine. While couture designers are only allowed a brief moment on the catwalk at the end of the show, we are happy to put the two creators of the FK 6725 in the limelight: Jørgen Kastholm was a blacksmith before he studied furniture design with the great Finn Juhl in Copenhagen, where he met a young carpenter named Preben Fabricius and realized that they were both into minimalism, according to the motto: the simpler, the better.

In 1961, they opened a design studio together, and four years later German manufacturer Alfred Kill discovered a few of their pieces while strolling through the furniture fair in Fredericia in Denmark. Kastholm and Fabricius were very hesitant about industrial production, but when Kill offered each of them 2,500 Marks a month, they gave in and moved to the factory near Fellbach in Stuttgart. There they created the FK 6725 in steel and leather, which has sometimes been referred to as the Tulip Chair, then again as the Bird Chair. The two designer friends had a fall out in 1968, after which Kastholm became a design professor and continued to work on office furniture. He may well have seen Meryl Streep in his chair before he died in 2007.

Whether her role model Anna Wintour has a thing for seating furniture is not known, but many have tried to kick the legs from under her chair, if you believe the tabloids. On pictures that show her in her home office during the Covid-19 shutdown, she sits in sweatpants on a rather uncomfortable-looking wooden chair that she might have borrowed from her dining room. At this point, we urgently recommend that she try out the FK 6725. Two icons would have found each other. By the way, at over 70 years of age, Wintour has taken over the post of *Vogue*'s Global Editorial Director. The dead always live longer, and some never die. Like true design classics.

Created a legendary toy series almost by accident: As a student Renate Müller sewed animals out of sugar sacks, the rest is (as they say) history.

Renate Müller | 1967
Rupfentiere

Most people are not fans of rough textures, but in this case, it is actually one of our protagonists' most important personality traits. It goes without saying that hippos, elephants, and turtles take a back seat to all the smooth, sophisticated artworks so often produced these days. This is actually a perfect example of how real class sometimes goes unrecognized, like so many other things in life. These thick-skinned beasts are, in fact, heavyweights in the design world, and connoisseurs shell out thousands of dollars for them. Provided, of course, that R & Company, the exclusive New York art gallery of contemporary design, has them on hand. What sets the animals apart is that they have a hint of Bauhaus, whose ideals famously lay in design simplicity, functionality, and the use of natural materials.

Before you turn up your nose at the creatures and toss them willy-nilly into the toy chest, you might want to spare a glance for Denmark, where thousands of grown-ups keep Kay Bojesen's wooden monkeys perching on their shelves. Hello-oh! The jute beasts may be toys, but they were never intended to be a child's stuffed animal. At first, their creator, Renate Müller, viewed them as little more than practice pieces. In the 1960s, she studied design with Assistant Professor Helen Haeusler in the toy capital of Sonneberg, Germany. As a self-professed Bauhaus fan, Haeusler thought nothing of giving her students a practice piece that would be right at home in the nursery. She stocked her classroom with dozens of burlap sugar sacks to be used as source material, and her protégés sewed and crafted their pieces. However, it wasn't until after graduation that Renate Müller finally became a kind of zookeeper. She sewed a veritable menagerie of creatures, which her traditionalist father eyed with skepticism. In the toy paradise of Sonneberg, people tended to prefer soft and fuzzy over rough jute-covered wood shavings. Renate Müller exhibited her first critters at the Leipzig Trade Show in the spring of 1967 under the theme:

69

"Rough, but with heart." They were granted permission to leave the GDR and travel to West Germany, where, to Müller's irritation, they were put up for sale under such silly names as Mocky, Mossy, and Flossi. The designer was far happier when her jute animals traveled all the way to Japan. They had long since proven to be ideal therapy animals for children, thanks to their tactile and stimulating surfaces. Even better, they withstood rough handling, tolerated being punched, pulled, and pushed about, and even refused to be crushed when sat on by a tiny tot. Normally, design is easy on the eye and hard on the pocketbook. However, these works of art healed the whole body and, priced at 150 marks each, did not break the bank. Early on, they could be found in hospitals, doctor's offices, and kindergartens, while today they turn up in museums. Müller's crowning achievement is certainly not the "Little Bee," the only one of Müller's work to be lent by the Palace of the Young Pioneers in Oberhof, GDR, before German reunification. Instead, it is her contribution to the Century of the Child exhibit at MoMA in New York.

Born in 1945, Renate Müller has enjoyed a long career as an artist, exhibiting enormous carpets at the Biennale in Venice, for instance. She still sews individual animals as a kind of object art. From time to time, her work is hawked on eBay for horrendous prices, which she find disturbing. When someone sent her a mouse-eaten piece for repair, she slammed the box shut again in disgust. "It's quite nice when the animals arrive with the scents of domestic life, because you can always pass them on to someone else," she says. "But you can't possibly give them to a child in such a funky condition!" Sometimes even the love of animals has its limits.

The *Rupfentiere* were intended as therapeutic toys and were used in the German Democratic Republic mainly in schools and children's hospitals.

Ingmar Relling | 1965
Siesta Chair

Being the baby of the family can have definite advantages if you are treated with loving care and pampered by your parents and older siblings. But sometimes, the youngest also stands in the shadow of her older brothers and sisters, unable to take her place in the sun. In fact, it can be quite chilly in the shade. It's easy to fall through the cracks, get lost, be overlooked. When you think about Scandinavian design, what comes to mind are a whole lot of high-profile Danish, Swedish, and Finish architects, but where, you might ask, can Norway be found? Oddly enough, the country has never called out "over here!" when prizes for outstanding designs were handed out. On class photos, it never insisted on sitting in the front row. Or even to be in the picture at all. Norway never even realized that the school photographer was in the building. For decades, it simply focused single-mindedly on what it supposedly did best: producing and exporting raw materials. Processing these materials seemed not to matter at all or at least not to be worth mentioning. Of course, the Norwegians wove beautiful linen cloth, built fine furniture out of its wood, threw ceramic vases on the wheel. But to boast about their achievements or loudly proclaim them to the world? Anything but that! Norwegian interior design professionals readily admit that their compatriots have little talent for self-promotion. Good quality speaks for itself, so goes the thinking in the far north. Nice. And, sadly, fundamentally wrong.

This Norwegian armchair is considered an important representative of Scandinavian design and has received several awards.

Armchair 189

That's why we may trace the origin of many a pretty piece to Scandinavia, while placing it in the wrong corner of the region. Where do you think the Stokke Tripp Trapp highchair comes from? It's Norwegian, the brainchild of Peter Opsvik. Take the word *hygge*. Today, it evokes a sense of Scandinavian lifestyle par excellence and, taken on its own, represents a definitively Danish attitude toward life. And yet it has its roots in Norway. The word derives from *hyggia*, which means wellbeing, and it emigrated to Denmark via Sweden only in the 19th century. There was not real need for it in the land of Hurtigruten. After all, they had *kos* (cozy togetherness), from which other words are derived: *peiskos* (the comfort of a roaring fire), *hyttekos* (the cozy atmosphere of a rustic cabin), and, let's not forget, *hjemmekos* (the warm feeling of being home).

Interesting fact: Norwegian designers themselves are partly to blame when people attribute their ideas to other countries. Many of them work for Danish and Finnish labels, such as Muuto, Iittala, and Hay. At the furniture trade show in Milan, they gather in fascinating groups that could easily hold their own against competition from neighboring countries, including the Klubben Kollektiv and Norway Says.

Norway does indeed have a voice, but always talks in a whisper. And so we are happy to hand over the megaphone. Legendary Norwegian designs include the Dokka pendant lamp, designed by Birger Dahl back in the 1950s. And what may well be the pièce de résistance: The Siesta armchair, which the Norwegian architect and designer Ingmar Relling created for the Westnofa company in 1965, together with his son Knut. To this very day, it remains one of the most important representatives of Scandinavian design. In Copenhagen, the chair is regarded as a kind of response to the work of Danish designer Hans J. Wegner, but Relling & son have always been able to speak for themselves without being mentioned in the same sentence with a Dane. Indeed, the Siesta armchair made waves in its day as a popular export in addition to the usual suspects of salmon, oil, and natural gas. More than one million pieces have been sold in over 50 countries. Including the United States, where former President Jimmy Carter once furnished the White House with as many as 16 Siesta lounge chairs. The man had a real sense of style. And an appreciation for quiet time.

The Siesta Chair quickly became an interior icon thanks to its details, harmonious proportions and durability.

FAILURE OR NOT?
Much ado about nothing, but enough to steam both users and the manufacturer.

Philippe Starck had obviously been paying attention when the Memphis style turned the design world upside down in the 1980s. After almost a decade, the colorful furniture and accessories cobbled together from geometric shapes were suddenly no longer perceived as crazy enfants terribles, but had arrived in the everyday life of the masses. His Hot Bertaa kettle hit the zeitgeist quite wonderfully in 1989 with its conical body, which seems to be pierced by a trumpet-like spout. Unfortunately, Hot Bertaa hit the mark pretty well in other respects, too: The hot water vapor was sometimes aimed directly at the user. In addition, there were a few other troubles with the everyday object, which was also no bargain: It was all too easy to burn your fingers on the aluminum body, and—this was also on the list of shortcomings—you could never tell how much water was actually in the Hot Bertaa. But we don't want to be picky now: Many competing models don't offer this service either. Starck's strong words, however, took his kettle ad absurdum: "I want to create things for buyers that they can really use, that are of outstanding quality, that help them, and that have no regard whatsoever for the prevailing zeitgeist," he had claimed. The fact that his Hot Bertaa actually became timeless, however, was more due to the fact that it was taken off the market again after around six years and only 25,000 copies. Manufacturer Alberto Alessi later called the kettle "our most beautiful fiasco." After all, you really couldn't deny the hot thing any wit, nor could you deny it an interesting design. If it were to meet Starck's other statement piece for Alessi, the Juicy Salif lemon squeezer (▶ p. 122), in some chic kitchen, both could lament each other's status as misunderstood art. And why not? Flops, for Alberto Alessi, are avowedly just proof of the triumph of creativity over mere commerce. When he joined the company founded by his grandfather in 1970, he asked Salvador Dalí, among others, to design a sculpture that would then go into production as a work of art for everyone. Dalí supplied a kind of giant stainless-steel surface with a golden comb from which a fishhook dangled. The fact that it remained a one-off piece was down to Alberto's father: He didn't believe in serial success and stopped the project. Nevertheless, the Alessi company is daring and believes in form, not pure functionality. Very Italian, one might say. *Fare bella figura*—looking good is everything.

Is that why Hot Bertaa failed? This is a matter of opinion. You're only dead when no one talks about you anymore. Seen in this light, the kettle is still pretty hot.

Philippe Starck | 1985

Hot Bertaa

71

Only 25,000 of the Alessi water kettles were produced.

Words are good weapons, but you can also stab yourself with them without any problem. Especially in times of so-called woke language regulations, which are all about who may be addressed when, how and in what way, which terms are on the no-go list, which jokes one should laugh at or, on the contrary, be outraged by. The woke word itself dates back to the 1930s, when it was used by African Americans to express awareness of social oppression and racism. So now let's try to approach the Nordic natives in a woke and politically correct way, whereby the blunders are about as wide spread as lakes in the Finnish landscape. The origin of the word is unclear, but one suspects that it could have something to do with a similar term for outlying areas, which would then brand the people so designated as country bumpkins or even outsiders. Another interpretation even locates the North Germanic word for rag (*Lappen*), and so it is little wonder that it was forbidden to use the word Laplander under penalty in 16th century Finland. But even the Sami, as the peoples are officially called today, still have the misnomer in their vocabulary—for those compatriots who keep reindeer. The matter therefore remains unsettled. The term Eskimo has been on the index for a long time anyway, supposedly Inuit is the only accepted alternative, although most people in Alaska prefer to be called Eskimo rather than Inuit. Especially since the word Eskimo has its bad reputation quite unjustifiably: that it supposedly means raw meat eater has long been disproved. The word is likely to mean either snowshoe weavers or "people who speak a different language".

Alvar Aalto | 1937

Waves

So, that's settled, and that also rehabilitates the famous Finnish architect Alvar Aalto, who in 1936 submitted his vases and bowls to a competition held by the Karhula-Iittala glass factory under the project title "Eskimoerindens Skinnbuxa", approximate translation: leather pants of a female Eskimo, and promptly took first place. The company immediately presented one of the revolutionary curved pieces at the Paris World Fair and used it to furnish the Savoy luxury restaurant in Helsinki, which Alvar and his wife Aino were in the process of delighting with their designs anyway. That's why the famous Alvar Aalto vase is also known today as "the Paris thing" or the "Savoy vase." Good thing: Its original designation, the one with the aboriginal woman's leg dress, was now truly unpronounceable.

There is hardly a piece by the great Finn that would have suited him more: Aalto liked to give his buildings sweeping lines so that they blended into the landscape. The vase, so wonderfully organic in form, symbolized the lakes of his homeland—and, incidentally, the name of the master himself: Aalto, after all, translates as wave.

It used to take seven glassblowers and up to 30 hours of work for a single one of the Aalto vases, and even today each piece is hand-blown in Iittala's workshops. Not too much fuss about a curve star in a class of its own, I would say.

Arne Jacobsen | 1958

Egg Chair

Even the most creative of geniuses weren't born artists. That's easy to forget once their names are so inextricably bound up with their works, but the journey from taking their first hesitant steps to immortality was a long one. They were often tempted by side streets and shortcuts, and it sometimes took a complete change in direction for them to arrive at their final mastery. This is true of many disciplines. Soccer icon Franz Beckenbauer first studied to be an insurance salesman, the great Sean Connery worked as a milkman and lifeguard, and painter Gerhard Richter, who has been ranked by "Kunstkompass" as the world's most important artist for the past 16 years, actually wanted to be a forest ranger but wasn't strong enough—he was "weighed and found wanting," so to speak, which was fortunate for art fans. And when top architect Arne Jacobsen finished school, he also had something else in mind. He wanted to paint with brush on canvas, but his father said no, he thought it was a highly unprofitable profession. Arne's abrupt act of covering the lushly patterned carpets in his parents' house with whitewash did nothing to make the father more receptive to his offspring's ideas. Jacobson Senior thought his son should first learn to draw and recommended that he study architecture. That sounded reasonable enough—and very Scandinavian. It was the perfect decision for Junior. One of his first sketches, a circular "house of the future" with a helipad and jetty, became an instant masterpiece. From then on, his business boomed. He built apartment buildings, city halls, theaters, a beach complex, a gas station, and finally a hotel with all the fixings. In 1958, he designed every last detail of the SAS Royal Hotel in Copenhagen, right down to the silverware in the restaurant. The sculptured chairs with interesting names like Egg and Swan were the real stars of the SAS inventory and went on to became icons, divas that spoke for themselves. They were and still are ahead of their time, not unlike Jacobsen's iconic Series 7 chairs. Actually, he created all these pieces during the same period. The most intriguing feature of the leather Egg chair is the fact that the entire cover is all one piece. How did Jacobsen manage it? He must have found the Egg of Columbus.

73

Fritz Hansen still produces the world-famous chair under the name „Egg™". Here it can be seen together with its siblings, the „Swan" and the „Drop".

198   Armchair

At first, of course, the citizens of Copenhagen saw only the boxy hotel structure that the master had plopped down in their city and voted it Copenhagen's ugliest building. For some reason, Jacobsen's designs for public buildings never did appeal to popular taste. In Germany, the citizens of Mainz still resent him today for his city hall with its gray facade that looks like bars, and it's likely that the three looming residential towers on the south beach of the Island of Fehmarn are tolerated only because the entire ensemble is protected by landmark status as a complete work of art. Although in some cases we have to wonder what the old master was thinking, the citizens of Copenhagen appreciate his smaller accomplishments, like the rich interior life of the hotel block and the aforementioned Egg and Swan, the originals of which can still be found in the hotel lobby. And if you ever check into the SAS, ask for room 606. It's the only room that's still furnished according to the original design with, of course, an Egg chair covered in verdant green.

Would Arne Jacobsen have been happier as a painter? There was at least one alternative he wouldn't have minded. He said that in his next life, he wanted to be a gardener—and then retreated to the garden of his (self-)designed town house in Klampenborg.

He actually wanted to become a painter: Designer Arne Jacobsen. Urged by his father to study, he became one of the world's most important architects and designers.

74

Ron Arad | 1994

Bookworm

Unfulfilled dreams can be crushing, and beneath their weight, some people have no other choice than to take the plunge and start a new life. There are plenty of stories about women and men who went out to buy cigarettes and never came back. Austrian singer and composer Udo Jürgens even wrote a song about it: "Ich war noch niemals in New York" (I've never been to New York). Longing for freedom and escape, his dubious protagonist runs out the front door and into the street and almost, but not quite, flags down a cab to take him to the airport so that he can embark on a big adventure in the Big Apple. Although there aren't many people with the courage to change their lives in an instant, we know that designer Ron Arad was one of them.

In 1979, he'd just completed his degree in architecture and started his first job in London. One day he took his lunch break—and simply never came back. "I love architecture," he later said, "but I don't love the profession so much because it's a profession of compromises. There are always lots of negotiations—with the fire brigade, with the police, with the contractor, with the neighbors, with the husband, with the wife." Arad wanted to do his own thing, not to have to explain what he was doing to anyone or have to justify it. So he quit, gave up a steady salary, and started creating objects.

The first was the Rover chair, made of pipe couplings and a car seat that he found in a scrapyard. Not many years later, he was already so famous that he was asked to contribute to an exhibition celebrating the tenth anniversary of the Centre Georges-Pompidou in Paris. Arad showed up with a kind of machine that pressed chairs into cubes and then used them to build a wall. Wherever consumer critique goes, art will follow, and maybe radical actions like this one are the path to immortality. But even artistic designers have to eat, and Arad needed something he could sell. In 1993, he wanted to pick up his daughter at school but it was pouring rain, so he lingered a moment in his car and drew an S-shaped line on the fogged-up windshield. It was his first sketch of a bookshelf that he then made at home by bending a steel coil into shape. The prototype of "This Mortal Coil" still hangs on his living room wall—shelves without a single straight line, of any conceivable length, basically without limits. "A new piece of furniture that was born without any labor pain," said its creator. "Just like, 'Why don't I do that?' And there it is."

This innovative shelf was the big brother of the Bookworm created in 1994, which the Italian furniture label Kartell soon started producing out of plastic—making it more attractive but no less bendable. It was Arad's biggest commercial success to date. As he once said, "Art is recognizing which ideas are worth following up." That fateful lunch break—wasn't it also a moment of recognition? Strictly speaking, it wasn't yet art, but it was Ron Arad's basis for becoming an artist.

It stylishly displays books during a reading break: the famous Bookworm.

The piece bears Le Corbusier's initials with LC—but it was Charlotte Perriand who drove the lounger's development.

Of course, you know immediately who you are looking at here: When it comes to Corbusier's chaise lounge, the LC4, the L stands for Le, the C for Corbusier, just to dispel any doubts. Indeed, the great master had once again pulled it off—but by that I'm not referring to the design, but to the fact that the piece would immediately and forever be associated with his name. The problem was that the "resting machine," as Le Corbusier described the lounger, had not been designed by him at all, or at least not exclusively: It was primarily the work of Charlotte Perriand, a young Frenchwoman who had started working in his Paris architectural office. She is the one who commissioned the upholstery and cushions and tinkered with the first prototypes in her studio in Saint-Sulpice. Le Corbusier and his cousin Pierre Jeanneret would come by to have a look every now and then. A few times they gave it the thumbs down, but at some point they were finally satisfied with Charlotte's work. And thus it was allowed to participate in the Paris Autumn Salon. Charlotte was also the one who persistently searched for an investor until she was able to convince the Thonet brothers of the novelty of the lounger.

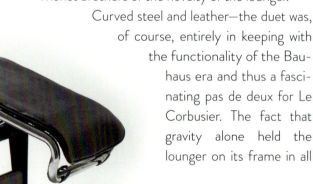

Curved steel and leather—the duet was, of course, entirely in keeping with the functionality of the Bauhaus era and thus a fascinating pas de deux for Le Corbusier. The fact that gravity alone held the lounger on its frame in all

Charlotte Perriand | 1928

LC4 Chaise Lounge

positions must have delighted him. And that the stroke of genius was ultimately attributed to him must have pleased him as well. Incidentally, the architect, who was born Charles-Édouard Jeanneret-Gris, had based his pseudonym on the name of his great-grandmother, Lecorbésier, and the word *corbeau* for raven. Ravens are known to be extremely clever, masters of advance planning, and amazingly good at waiting for the right opportunity. Whether they are also stubborn, I don't know, but what is certain is that Perriand's lounge always remained a chair in Le Corbusier's eyes—because he recognized only chairs as an architectural achievement; he considered sofas to be too bourgeois.

Anyone who buys an LC4 today is therefore shelling out a few grand to officially own a Le Corbusier. Italian manufacturer Cassina had already taken the lounge under its wing in 1964, but at least they did not forget Charlotte Perriand in the end. To mark her 110th birthday in 2014, the Italians treated her to a symbolic laurel wreath in the form of a few letters: A special edition by Cassina and Louis Vuitton not only features the finest saddle leather, but also her initials with the name LC4 CP.

But let's be honest: The baby has long since fallen into the well, the fish has been gutted, or whatever other metaphors you might find to describe a successful—not hostile—but nevertheless cunning takeover. After all, you can't blame Le Corbusier for not wanting to kill the goose that laid the golden eggs. Who wouldn't have done the same?

Jonathan Ive | 1997

Apple iMac

No, the computer has not lost its way in the ranks of the venerable classics, it has honestly earned its place. Creativity always has to do with openness, aesthetics knows no closed areas, so there you go. And anyway, as Apple founder Steve Jobs once said so beautifully: "I want Apple's design to be not only the best within the personal computer sector, but the absolute best within the whole world." We gladly accept such statements as an invitation to review them, and then we mentally travel to Cupertino in Silicon Valley, where an American success story took its course in the 1980s. Elsewhere, companies hang giant portraits of the company's founders on their walls or host elaborate events to get their employees in line. Steve Jobs put a grand piano and a motorcycle in the company headquarters. He wanted the products from his company to be as beautiful and sexy as they were. The only problem was that these were computers, and until then they had not necessarily been associated with lifestyle.

But that could be changed. Even with the first Macintosh, Steve Jobs drove his designers crazy. Sometimes he thought the thing was too bulky, then he demanded more curves or didn't like the proportions. The case of Apple's first model underwent several redesigns until the master was satisfied. Jobs obviously always knew what he didn't want, but it wasn't

The new iMac. Now in five flavours. Think different.

"Collect all five"—Apple was never at a loss for bold announcements in advertising. There are said to be people who actually bought all five iMacs, just because of the color.

until Jonathan "Jony" Ive came into the Apple universe in 1992 that a kind of creative mastermind really grasped his boss's understanding of style.

Until then, Ive had been exercising his creativity mostly on sinks, bathtubs and toilets, but now Jobs' genius and Ive's design wit set off on a highly creative pas de deux. The first iMac in 1997 changed the perception of computers forever. The partly colorful, partly transparent box drove out any gray noise from the computer, looked more lifestyle than work and even had something cuddly. "Think different" was the new slogan from Apple.

From then on, not only the technology industry lurked for innovations from Cupertino, but also the design-savvy public. Product presentations were applauded like sensational creations by great fashion designers on the catwalks in Milan or Paris. That's exactly what Jobs wanted: "We'll make the buttons on the screen look so good you'll want to lick them." The fancy computer cube three years later was a giftedly stylish design, affectionately called the Apple Toaster because of the vertically placed disk drive. Well, as a computer the thing flopped, but as an object it was celebrated and even moved into New York's Museum of Modern Art—into the showrooms, not the accounting department, mind you. With the first iPod, Ive switched to pure purism in 2001—and revealed a secret: From childhood on he had been an avowed fan of Braun designer Dieter Rams.

And that was the end of it: The famous Apple design actually has German roots, and anyway: Didn't Walter Gropius evoke the important alliance of technology and art in 1923 during the move of the Bauhaus to Dessau? Exactly. By the way, it is more than obvious that the iPod had relatives in Germany: Just take a look at Braun's pocket radio T3 from 1958!

Meanwhile, Jonathan Ive is no longer at Apple, but the force is with him: His aesthetics are loved by around 1.4 billion people. That is, by everyone who has a Mac or an iPhone. Dieter Rams, by the way, owned both an iPod and an iPhone. His disciple Ive had given them to him. That's also a kind of royalty payment.

It is actually amazingly easy to make money. In the evolutionary history of millionaires, there are plenty of examples of people who became rich with a simple idea, entirely without risk. One example is the advertising website of student Alex Tew, who sold a million pixels at the price of one dollar each. Gary Dahl, who has been hawking rocks as low-maintenance pets since 1975 and seems to be raking in the dough without end. Or Josh Opperman, whose broken engagement gave him the idea of creating an Internet marketplace for used wedding and engagement rings, which has since been snapped up for several million. These guys have easily left us in the dust. And so the perplexing question remains: Why didn't you think of it yourself?

Arne Jacobsen | 1961

Design Letters

It's a question that could easily be asked in light of the success of graphic designer Mette Thomsen. She loved typefaces of all kinds and has inspired many other people with her passion. Typography, the art of designing with fonts, is after all a huge trend, both in the interior design sector and in the DIY sector. People like to paint in black, and do so with growing pleasure; there are countless fonts to choose from, some of them with appealing names ranging from Adelle to Wiesbaden Swing to Zentenar Fraktur. With Google Fonts, Google alone offers around a thousand fonts. Nobody needs them? That isn't true: The way letters are presented is communication in its purest form, and some fonts are really famous. Just think of the lettering for Nivea cream, for example, or the one for Nutella, or the Basic Commercial typeface used for the signs in the New York subway system. When a font and a product form a successful alliance, the advertisers have done something absolutely right.

And if a handful of letters become icons, at some point you might automatically ask yourself who designed them. Or in other words, whether at some point some well-known name had taken an interest in letters. Mette Thomsen wanted to know exactly that, so she did a little research and found a typeface created in 1937 by her compatriot, Arne Jacobsen—the man behind the Egg chair, the Swan chair, and the SAS Hotel in the Danish capital. Incidentally, he originally created the typeface for the city hall he designed in Aarhus. Tracking down the set of letters in the Danish Royal Library in Copenhagen was one thing, but negotiating the rights with the architect's descendants was another. Thomsen either made a good case, had money, or both. In any case, she founded Design Letters in 2010 and printed letters on mugs, plates, posters, vases, etc., and became a bit famous herself. And rich, I suspect. But that doesn't make others any poorer, because now anyone can buy a genuine piece of design that embodies the master's work one hundred percent: restrained, clear, straightforward. AJ, as he lived and breathed.

77

As early as 1937, Arne Jacobsen threw the first hand drawings of typographic symbols and letters onto paper; the finished set radiates dignity and conciseness. However, they were not kissed awake and marketed until 2010 by Jacobsen's compatriot, the graphic designer Mette Thomsen.

The Antelope Chair, once designed for the Festival of Britain, with its playful sculptural form was a harbinger of a new optimism in the postwar era in Great Britain.

Great Britain's garden art is legendary, and for many the English lawn has become an unrivaled ideal. Anyone who despairs because their own grass struggles to grow and is nowhere close to being as beautifully dense as on the estates of the various earls and dukes should rest assured that it's because of the island location. The British may not have the best weather, but they definitely have the perfect climate for lawns: mild winters, rather cool summers, and rain throughout the year.

Ernest Race | 1951

Antelope Chair

English park culture produced a different, but no less remarkable offspring back in the 17th century with an innovation called the ha-ha, or sometimes the a-ha. It is a landscape design element that incorporates a ditch with one vertical side to create an insurmountable barrier that eliminates the need for traditional walls or fences. Thanks to this sunken design, the landscape appears wide and airy with uninterrupted views.

As a result, the wife of Lord Perceval, Earl of Egmont, must have enjoyed splendid panoramic views when, seated on a Windsor chair, she was carried by her footmen through one of the many parks in the county of Berkshire in 1724. Windsor chairs were common in many households at the time. The small chairs were considered rather simple and cheap, and when used outdoors they were painted green. That lady's lofty seat might well have been an ancestor of the first garden chairs.

In the early 19th century, people were already enjoying their five o'clock tea on simple, weatherproof chairs, which soon became available in a practical folding version. It was not until the middle of the 20th century that the garden chair business truly began to flourish. The trend began when travelers to Italy returned home with the optimistic idea of spending a little more time outdoors despite the weather. The war was a thing of the past, and although swords could not be turned into plowshares, the aluminum of British war planes had certainly been reworked into dining room furniture. And instead of having to think about air raids, people were once again enjoying light and breezy hours outside in gardens.

In 1951, the Festival of Britain also celebrated the revival of joie de vivre. With the Antelope Chair, Ernest Race had contributed the perfect piece of outdoor furniture to the festival: lively, playful, and somehow optimistic. At the same time, it was highly British, full of references to English history: a touch of wing chair, a hint of Windsor—the Antelope chair simply had it all. Whether its ball feet already anticipated the molecular structures of the future, as the Council of Industrial Design claimed to have observed—perhaps so. In any case, the curvaceous garden chair was subsequently put to work in prominent places—including on the terrace of the Royal Festival Hall.

Could a chair be more English? Probably not. The elegant outdoor standout even carries a sense of tradition—it's still made in the same Gloucestershire factory as it always has been. Another noteworthy feature of the British design furniture is a profound knowledge of its place: Its seat is perforated to allow rainwater to drain away.

FAILURE OR NOT?
So sweet it gives you a toothache. For European interiors rather indigestible.

Jackie Rice, his teacher at design school in New York, certified her student from New Jersey as having zero talent and advised him to become a lawyer instead, but for heaven's sake he should keep his hands off arts and crafts. The only problem was that since attending a summer camp at the tender age of twelve, Jonathan Adler could hardly be lured away from the potter's wheel and wouldn't even think of giving up his clay experiments. So he kept going and even landed the luxury department store Barneys as a customer. In 1998 he opened his first store in SoHo, sold cushions designed together with Peruvian craftsmen and scribbled his first sketches for matching sofas on paper. At some point, he had everything in his repertoire as a designer that you could put in your house. "A car," he says, "I'd like to do that someday, too."

Jonathan Adler | 2012

Pompidou

Until then, he's probably doing what he's been doing all along: designing things that are out of the ordinary. That catch the eye. "Minimalism is crap," is his very favorite credo, and so the most significant part of his oeuvre can be described something like this: pottery animal figures, bowls with faces, velvet chairs with shiny stainless-steel bases. Brass, gold—and yes, with pleasure also some bling-bling. Don't you dare call it kitsch. Adler actually maintains a not entirely serious list of words that are better not used in his presence—including substitute words. Fancy, fresh, posh, Hollywood style—he likes that much better. Or, best of all: Modern American Glamour. He is loved for this, sits on Oprah Winfrey's talk show, has been allowed to furnish pompous hotels like the Parker Palm Springs, writes design books, and designs for his own 22 stores. There are plenty of industry insiders who hate him. But there are also those who think his stylistic madness is a kind of genius after all. Either way, there's no getting around him. Adler is one of the most famous designers in the world.

His style always looks a bit like luxury, which should be recognized as such. Mannered, flashy—and somehow also funny. I'll tell you: A piece of Jonathan Adler here and there—that can look really good. A nice complement to the Mid-Century or Nordic style, which are not quite dissimilar in many ways.

The porcelain vase Pompidou clearly belongs in the temperate climate zone of his very personal creative map, so to speak. A beautiful piece with psychedelic graphic pattern full of 1970s flair. And since its creator always gives a good story, it puts a surefire communication tool on your sideboard. But Pompidou is also a bit of a good deed: Adler cooperates with the non-profit organization Aid to Artisans, which helps artisans in poorer countries earn a living. A large part of Adler's products, including the Pompidou, are therefore made in Peru.

Anyone who Googles the name of Jonathan's design professor Jackie Rice today, Jonathan Adler once remarked with a smile not entirely free of schadenfreude, "first finds her in reports about my person." As a footnote in the incredible success story of potter and star designer Jonathan Adler.

80

Sori Yanagi | 1954

Butterfly

Fusion is one of the words that reflects today's zeitgeist. After all, it's not about a formal connection, but rather a kind of pas de deux between two different styles. Fine restaurants serving fusion cuisine usually feature a delicious combination of two national cuisines; in interior design, an imaginary creature called Japandi is the product of Japan's fruitful encounter or fusion with a predominantly Scandinavian West. Purity of style is out, and it certainly isn't woke. But that was by no means always the case.

Japan in particular kept its distance from the West for a long time; during the Tokugawa period between 1600 and 1868, Nippon isolated itself completely. At times, as a precaution, ships large enough to reach other countries were not even allowed to be built there. It was not until the Meiji era that people began to regard the West with greater sense of curiosity; an American named Commodore Matthew Perry pushed aside the shoji screens, so to speak. Perhaps it was due to pent-up demand on both sides; in any case, Western and Eastern cultures soon enjoyed a busy back-and-forth, a lively exchange between the continents.

Against the backdrop of World War II, Charlotte Perriand, Corbusier's assistant, was invited to Japan to serve as an advisor on industrial design. Perriand boarded the Hakusan

Maru to embark on her journey and landed in the Empire of the Rising Sun in 1940. She had been recommended by the architect Junzo Sakakura, who had spent a number of instructive years in Corbusier's studio in Paris before opening his own office in Tokyo. That is where, in turn, the young Sori Yanagi worked, and the Frenchwoman now had Yanagi by her side as a translator and assistant. What she brought back from Japan was the love of emptiness, which she had discovered there. Perriand had come to understand that emptiness is not nothingness, but rather that it represented "the possibility of moving" and that "emptiness contains everything." In turn, she encouraged the Japanese to reflect upon their own creativity: "They were so focused on their traditions or else trapped into copying objects they had seen in magazines," she later explained in her autobiography. "I encouraged them to create new objects."

Perriand's assistant, Yanagi, must have listened to her particularly well. In 1954, he thus combined the best of both worlds to create a true masterpiece, the Butterfly Stool. He used the technique of bending plywood, which had so recently been celebrated in the West, to impose an extremely elegant and profoundly Japanese shape on the wood. Now for a quick sidelong glance at the timeline: It was that same year that Max Bill created the upright, straight Ulm stool (▶ p. 242) some 10,000 kilometers away—talk about an alternative concept! And what a terrific example of cultural differences. The Butterfly Stool was an award winner at the 1957 Milan Triennale. Fusion, of course. It's simply that the word hadn't yet come into fashion back then.

The Butterfly Stool by Sori Yanagi uniquely combines Eastern forms with the plywood molding technique developed by Charles and Ray Eames.

Most people prefer to keep their bedtime stories to themselves, with one obvious exception being the stars of various trash TV programs which generate ratings with revelations and unvarnished conversations. And of course pacifists like John Lennon and Yoko Ono, who nestled into the sheets of the Amsterdam Hilton Hotel in 1969 to improve the world in a highly publicized way. At the time, bed-ins became silent protest actions of the youth, horizontal political declarations. In bed, the view of the world inevitably changes because the perspective is different. And even in the smallest of private spaces, hardly anything is more relaxing than simply stretching out comfortably under the covers. Architectural historian Beatriz Colomina of Princeton University, however, believes that the bed is capable of much more: She has called for the century of the bed. Digitization is changing our living space, she says; already 80 percent of young New Yorkers work from their beds. Colomina also called for bed-ins, where she invited a few smart thinkers to her favorite piece of furniture and held equally smart discussions with them.

Peter Maly | 1983

Maly Bed

Designers don't seem to be joining in on singing the praises of beds, otherwise there would have to be more like them amongst the world's most important design pieces, wouldn't there? Here's the thing: Creative people can't really let their imagination run wild when it comes to beds. The dimensions are quite strict, and so is the shape—you just have to fit a mattress in it. The bed may be a marvelous way to play, but it does not offer very much flexibility when it comes to the development process.

Nevertheless, Peter Maly from Hamburg achieved tremendous success with his eponymous bed for Ligne Roset in 1983. It was very simple, very low, but equipped with a special feature: Fixed cushions that could be inserted anywhere other than just at the head of the bed. This allowed it to also be used as a substitute for an armchair, a sofa, or a place for dinner. When the furniture became a bit of a slow seller, the company discontinued it until owner Michel Roset reached out to Maly with a suggestion: "The bed is still beautiful," he supposedly said. "But if you take another shot at it, just don't make it as big as an aircraft carrier." Maly tweaked it a little here and there, making it height-adjustable, while of course keeping its special touches. And although the times may have changed, box spring mattresses will still not fit because they are not part of Peter Maly's world. As a designer who actually started out as an editor at the lifestyle magazine *Schöner Wohnen*, Maly considers them to be a fad and has a definite opinion about that: "Making products fashionable, subjecting them to a pace that is far too fast, is downright irresponsible." The man who modeled his first groundbreaking design for a chair, the Zyklus for Cor, on his daughter's doll chair, is conservative in the best sense of the word. And thus, again, completely in tune with the times.

„My work is characterized by the search for an expressive form, which, however, should not push itself into the front despite the greatest possible independence." Peter Maly

It was sometime in 1965 when, during a visit to the British capital, Italian upholstered furniture manufacturer Aurelio Zanotta plopped himself down onto a sofa that the lively art director Willie Landels had assembled from pieces of foam. Those present—all the glittering personalities of Swinging London, such as Princess Margaret and her husband, the Earl of Snowdon, as well as the future shoe God Manolo Blahnik—saw only a sofa, but Aurelio Zanotta recognized it as the "design of the future." It was frameless, set no boundaries, and thus got by without any guidance; it was completely unconventional. It was a perfect fit for a time when a generation of wannabe revolutionaries was looking for new directions, unwilling to be constrained and constricted.

Zanotta was an astute observer. And he was well aware that interior design is never just a fad, but also a reflection of society. The answers to questions concerning future interior design trends often last only a few months; their half-life is modest. On the other hand, it is always exciting to wonder about the direction in which architecture and design are traveling on the vast ocean of possibilities. Where we are headed and what we secretly dream of has always been reflected at some point in how we live. And a trend has always been followed by its countermovement: Art nouveau and art deco were followed by the Bauhaus style, which was streamlined for functionality; the well-behaved Mid-century modern movement was followed by the wild, colorful, and soft late 1960s and 1970s.

De Pas, D'Urbino, Lomazzi and Scolari | 1967

Blow

Aurelio Zanotta sensed the new vibes in London back then; something tremendous was in the air, and the DIY sofa by Landels seemed to get to the heart of it. Zanotta had it produced as a "throw away" couch in a variety of colors—and it was the first of many subsequent structureless pieces of furniture for which the label became famous. Zanotta dared to take a

82

chance and drove a stake into the ground around which the less daring gave a wide berth. In 1967, four young architects—Jonathan De Pas, Donato D'Urbino, Paolo Lomazzi, and Carla Scolari—found in Zanotta the perfect producer for their design of an inflatable sofa and armchair, Blow. Blow was furniture for cuddling, but unfortunately it was so susceptible to damage inflicted by cat claws, sharp fingernails, or cigarettes that were parked too close to it that its packaging also included an air pump and a repair kit. It was because of its vulnerability that it was sent into a forced retirement just a few years later, before Zanotta ventured to reissue it in 1989.

In today's world, Blow would have deflated much earlier: Our values have changed—and so have the things we want to live with. Durability and sustainability are the criteria that determine our well-being. Blow was a nice accessory upon which hippies could sleep off an occasional LSD high. You might check your basement to see whether its clear plastic cover is still there. Back then you could buy it for 20 dollars, but today it easily fetches 50 times that. Nostalgia has its price... And, discreetly, doesn't ask about durability.

FAILURE OR NOT?
The Toucan has never outgrown its infancy and therefore did not go down well with adults.

When parents talk about the education of their children's tastes, they are usually referring to the all-out battle of broccoli, spinach, and carrots against ice cream, cookies, and gummy bears. Usually no one thinks about an early education in style; people most likely expect role models to serve yet again as instructors. But how can the younger generation be introduced to style? And should we even do it at all? You can look at this question philosophically or from a simple economic perspective. After all, children are not only the consumers of the future, they are also already an important sales market in their own right, with many brands throwing themselves at their feet. So let's diplomatically sidestep the question a bit by saying that although children don't need design, it certainly can't hurt. Let's get down to business: The Panton Chair, the Barcelona chair, an offshoot of Arne Jacobsen's Series 7 chair, and even the Eiermann desk have long been available in mini versions for youngsters. The Eames Elephant was designed from the outset to amuse children, and Finnish architect Eero Aarnio followed up his cute pony stool with a puppy version in plastic for children's rooms. The stacking bed by Rolf Heide is also offered in a size for children. All these pieces have one thing in common: They not only speak the language of children, but they also seem surprisingly grown-up. Only in terms of colors do many manufacturers seem happy to accommodate the target group. The implications are clear: Some parents will eventually steal these nice pieces from their teenagers' rooms so they can make an impact in the living room. And the Eames Elephant probably never made it into the play area in the first place because it looked so damn good near the sofa.

Enea Ferrari | 1970

Toucan

There was never any danger of this with the Toucan lamp. It was the object artist Enea Ferrari from Verona, of all people, who came up with this colorful plastic thing in 1968. Until then, he had become known throughout the world for his monochrome white oil-on-wood art pieces. The Toucan is considered the world's first designer lamp for children and still fetches insane prices on the vintage market, but it comes with just one small question mark. It is possible that Ferrari wanted to make children's rooms around the world a little more colorful and fun. After all, there were apparently no limits to his imagination in the years that followed—he gave the world a Viking named Olaf, for example, and a red telephone booth as a lamp version. But if he had hoped to make a killing and fill a market niche with this children's lamp, the venture went rather awry. The Toucan never really caught on as a pet in Europe. After six years, its wings were clipped, or—more precisely—it disappeared from the lineup. In 2018, to mark its 50th birthday, it briefly took flight again as Cocorì in Ferrari's successor company Linea Zero under the aegis of his nephew Alessandro Zavater. All the same: highfliers do not look like this, sorry. But maybe it's simply the nature of the beast—after all, toucans are better at hopping than flying.

83

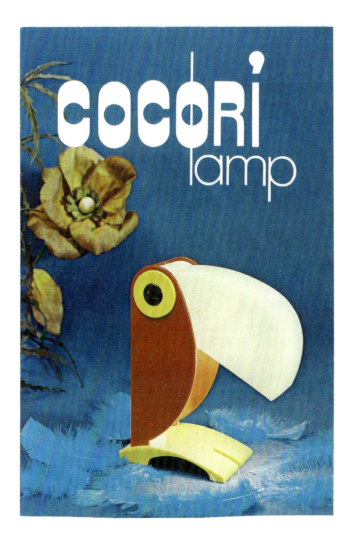

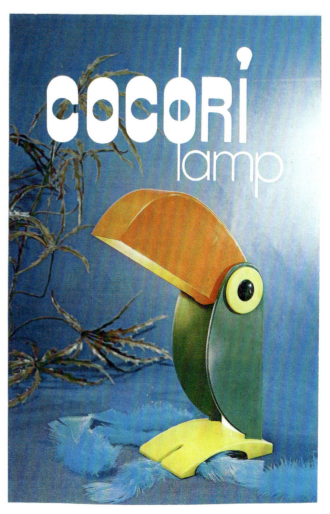

Conceived in the 1970s by Enea Ferrari and failed in its time, the Toucan lamp is now considered one of the most sought-after vintage objects on the auction market.

Faster and faster, more and more, the fashion market merry-go-round keeps spinning at full speed, now offering not just fast fashion but ultra-fast fashion. One of the biggest labels in this segment funnels 4,500 new pieces into stores each week. Instead of two collections—spring/summer and fall/winter—up to twelve collections are produced each year, an unfortunate development that not even the current sustainability trend has been able to halt. In the interior design world, we're not nearly as rushed, our trends tend to have a long half-life. People don't buy a new kitchen or sofa every year just because designers have chosen a different Pantone color of the year, and changeovers from one preference to another don't happen within a few months, but slowly worm their way in over a longer of period time. Up until the 1920s, vases were generally carved, ornately decorated, and full of romantic intrigue. Art Nouveau had long been in vogue. Even the Danish wholesale company Holst & Knudsen in Aarhus had been profiting from pieces that appealed to popular tastes since 1904, although the more austere Bauhaus style was already beginning to set the tone. Funnily enough, the company sourced its goods from Germany—which was a little like bringing coals to Newcastle, but when it came to industrial mass production, German prices were apparently unbeatable. Starting in 1930, high tariffs made imports impractical and Holst & Knudsen quickly changed course. They began to manufacture their own porcelain in a former sugar refinery in Kongens Lyngby in the suburbs of Copenhagen and, encouraged by their massive success, took an outrageous step. Under the new Lyngby Porcelæn label, they created a plain, grooved, white vase that wasn't even glazed. The response of the Danish public was lukewarm, so the company hastened to give the vase a few ornaments and decorative coatings. It wasn't until the 1950s that the plain version outstripped its ostentatious sibling. Suddenly its sober elegance was celebrated and it was held up as a style icon. In 1969, the company had to shut down for financial reasons and the vase was only available second-hand, but it made a brilliant comeback in 2012. Two men competed for the brand name and because Lyngby is an unsellable place name, both were authorized to manufacture the Lyngby vase. These fraternal twins can still be found on shelves today, one version from Lyngby by Hilfling in Denmark and the original model from Lyngby Porcelæn. Ever since the latter was acquired by the Rosendahl Design Group in 2016, the vase has been produced in Thuringia, Germany, giving the Dane dual citizenship. Its new colors change with the times but the grooves remain the same. It's a nice combination of trend and tradition. But the one thing it must have is the historic company monogram on its base.

Lyngby Porcelæn | 1930s
Lyngby Vase

It was the Dutchman Martinus Adrianus Stam who invented the first cantilever chair in 1926. A short time later, Marcel Breuer followed suit at the Bauhaus.

Smoking no longer tops the health hazard chart. It has been replaced by sitting. We spend an average of 14 hours a day on stools, chairs, and sofas. Orthopedists have their hands full trying to convince desk workers to stand up, stretch, and move their limbs once an hour. It's time that we engaged in what has infuriated generations of teachers when practiced by their students: dynamic sitting. At least fidgety children don't have back trouble.

Chairs that keep us from freezing in one position can be found in specialist stores, to be sure, although some of them look like they've sacrificed a lot of aesthetic form to achieve their function. But if you're willing to turn a blind eye, there's a more stylish option available: the cantilever chair. And it is indeed cantilevered, meaning that the seat extends out over a structure on the other end that gives it stability. But you won't find it in stores that specialize in ergonomic comfort. It's only available in well-stocked designer furniture stores. Just look for a chair that has no back legs.

Mart Stam | 1926

S 33

The concept of eliminating something that seems indispensable has long fascinated architects. In the 1920s, for example, Marcel Breuer became enamored of the idea of people one day sitting on columns of air. Dutch designer Mart Stam created a much more solid version in 1926 by welding together gas pipes to make a chair that had no hind legs. But the material was too rigid to allow a relaxing bounce. It annoyed his colleague, Bauhaus director Ludwig Mies van der Rohe, who didn't think the design was sophisticated enough. His then employee Sergius Ruegenberg told the following story in 1985. "In November 1926, Mies returned from Stuttgart and told us about Mart Stam and his chair idea. On the drawing board on the wall, Mies drew the Stam chair, right angles, starting from the top. He even added the pipe sleeves, saying, 'Ugly, so ugly with these sleeves. He could have at least rounded the edges.'" Drawing an arc, van der Rohe said, "That would look nicer," and with a single bold stroke, he invented a new chair, the MR 20. He presented his cantilever chair at an exhibition associated with his Weissenhof Siedlung in Stuttgart that focused on all sorts of experimental constructions.

Who invented it? It's a difficult question. Mart Stam was officially awarded the copyright by the German supreme court in 1932, but Mies van der Rohe could always claim that he brought flexibility to the cantilever chair and Breuer, who fitted his S 64 with wickerwork, could boast of a highly successful version. So in the end, the three musketeers of the cantilever chair all deserve their share of the credit. It's just a question of balance—which is what this chair is all about.

Nevertheless, we stubbornly stick to the originals. And once again we declare the S 33 to be the original, the father of all tube rockers. Which, of course, has itself become much more agile in the meantime. The manufacturer Thonet benefits from two versions of the competing trio: both Marcel Breuer's S 64 and Mart Stam's S 33 have been among its absolute bestsellers for years. Cantilever chairs at war with each other? Classics don't need that at all.

Colors can be hotly debated, and this was done in France towards the end of the 17th century in the form of impassioned pamphlets. These pamphlets addressed the question of what constituted the beauty of a painting. Was it brushwork, an accurate rendering of the subject matter, or color? In 1673, an essay by the art theoretician Roger de Piles ended the discussion with a paean to the luminous tones in the works of the famous painter Rubens. Color had won the debate. It has the best connections to our inner being, it touches our souls and seizes our feelings. It is not a fixed quantity; it is based on perception. In the end, it's all about rays of light, some of which are swallowed up by surfaces, while others are reflected. What researchers do know, however, is that colors cannot be understood by our mind, but only via the stimulus they exert on the nerve cells in our brains. They achieve their effects not only through the use of different pigments and mixtures, but above all through our experiences, memories, and emotions.

"Appearances are deceiving," is how Bauhaus teacher Josef Albers summed up this phenomenon. With his experimental series "Homage to the Square," he demonstrated that a color already has a different effect when it has to coexist with another color. It was simply "the most relative means of art."

Albers initially headed the stained glass workshop at the Bauhaus in Weimar, then took over Marcel Breuer's furniture workshop as well. In 1926, he emerged with a perfect alliance of the two disciplines: a set of nesting tables. Each table consisted of a clear lacquered oak structure with a red beech wood frame, which was covered with a colored glass top. It was a set of four nesting tables that Albers saw as more than just a decorative element for the Moellenhof House in Berlin. Instead, he viewed them as a textbook example of his color theory: The blue table looked completely different next to the red table than it did next to the yellow or turquoise table, and the light also had a significant impact on how each was perceived. Another good example of his theory is a viral phenomenon involving a dress that circulated on the Internet in 2015. The photograph of a striped dress became a phenomenon because people perceived it as either black and blue or—completely different—white and gold. It was an optical illusion—and a terrific reason for a lot of people to delve into neuroscientific phenomena.

Josef Albers | 1926

Nesting Tables

In fact, we all possess our own, often very personal color scale. Though it is true that our subconscious also associates a few fixed characteristics with certain color tones. Red has always been the color of power, of victory. Olympic teams that competed in this color have statistically won more often than others. In traffic, we usually come to a reverent stop at a red light. Red sounds the alarm, acts as a signal.

By contrast, our brain primarily associates the protective color of blue with trust and reliability. It also happens to be the favorite color of most people in the world. By the way, the RAL color palette was also created to ensure that we speak a common language when it comes to color, and the same goes for the American Pantone color system. But why do we always have to strictly catalog and pigeonhole everything? Colors, as the English writer James Henry Leigh Hunt once said, are the smiles of nature. That sounds more heartfelt. And thus actually closer to the essence of the different tones.

The nesting tables by Albers are currently being produced again by a traditional family business in the Erzgebirge using Italian glass. A piece of Bauhaus in both theory and practice. Powerful and convincing. By the way, you don't need a degree in color theory to come to this conclusion. Just style within your own four walls.

PARUPU
THE PaPER
PULP
CHAIR

FAILURE OR NOT? Sustainability is a science in itself. "Well-intentioned" is sometimes also "off the mark".

Claesson Koivisto Rune | 2009

Parupu

The new accolade in product design: environmentally friendly. Optionally, it may also be biodegradable or recyclable. All this is wonderful, and it was high time that the dainty ecological footprint was given the sex appeal of a desirable attribute. Someone came up with the great idea of fishing the plastic that kills turtles in the oceans and is now on our plates with every fish, out of the sea and making pretty things out of it. So we buy glasses, bracelets, sneakers, backpacks, but the real chic is the good conscience—and it just suits everyone.

The only problem with recycled ocean plastic is that it's usually only a tiny percentage that actually comes from the sea, and researcher Gilian Gerke of Magdeburg-Stendal University of Applied Sciences knew why after conducting a field test: "It's a lot of work and a hell of a lot of money," she discovered after fishing bags and nets out of the water herself with her students, cleaning them, sorting them and making things like letter openers out of them. Still, any push with environmentally friendly or recycled materials is a step in the right direction, even if the path to the sensible goal ends up being longer than one initially thought.

Joakim Nygren, a mechanical engineer at the time, also immediately took up the challenge when a fellow student slammed an egg carton on his desk and asked, "Can you make a chair out of it?" Nygren decided to make the project the subject of his master's thesis, got a Swedish pulp company on board—and Sweden's most famous designer trio, Ola Rune, Eero Koivisto and Mårten Claesson. The egg carton alone was not suitable as a stable basis, but when the wood fibers were mixed with a fully biodegradable plastic made from corn starch and heated, things looked differently. PLA or DuraPulp was the name of the newly developed material, of which the designer trio made a children's chair and presented the joint work at the Milan Furniture Fair 2009. The fact that children not only grow out of clothes, but also out of chairs, lost all horror with this chair: You could simply dispose of the Parupu in the compost.

The interest was gigantic. At first. Soon, a few experts began to make uncomfortable calculations: The parupu consisted largely of corn, which consumed vast amounts of water in cultivation and was actually supposed to feed people and animals, not just sit around stupidly in a chair. In addition, the production of PLA consumed more fossil energy than the production of polyethylene, heated the climate more than any fuel. The three designers Claesson, Koivisto and Rune, who otherwise gave us such wonderful lamps, chairs, sofas, already knew everything about style anyway. Since the Parupu, they also know a lot about sustainability. That can never hurt.

Max Bill's clock design thrives on reduction to the essentials.

Max Bill | 1961

Wristwatch

Reconciliation gifts given by many men: *rings and roses*. It's a pity that men so completely disregard the persuasive power of beautiful watches. Unfortunately, the three wouldn't work well together as an alliteration unless you decide to go with a Rolex. And it was a Rolex, by the way, that Marilyn Monroe gifted John F. Kennedy for his 45th birthday—along with her sultry performance of Happy Birthday that became so famous. Although her expensive gift was from the heart, it was all for naught—because "Jack" never wore it. In this respect, the golden Omega Constellation, which Elizabeth Taylor gave to her beloved husband Richard Burton, was a resounding success. Duchess Kate likely also admired the Cartier watch, model Ballon Bleu, which she received from William in 2014 for their third wedding anniversary. Incidentally, such timepieces are certainly stable in value, especially when a celebrity name is attached to their provenance: The Rolex Daytona that Joanne Woodward once gave to her racing enthusiast husband Paul Newman (engraving: "Drive Carefully. Me") sold for 17.8 million Dollars in 2017.

Rolex and the like are not exactly known for their restraint, but it is possible to use understatement to also make a splash in the business. In 1956, for example, architect and artist Max Bill was commissioned by the Black Forest clock and watch manufacturer Junghans to create a sky-blue kitchen clock with a 60-minute timer, an unadorned piece that focused strictly on the essentials. It still embodied the Bauhaus legacy, of course, which happened to be Bill's passion. The best thing that could be said about the clock was that you could tell the time at a glance. The hands were easily distinguishable, with a bar for the minutes and dashes for the hours. If you think the Arabic numerals are plain, you should take a look at number 4. This is where the master revealed his touch. You will not find anything comparable. An upside down chair? Perhaps. In a figurative sense, then, something you cannot rest on. It would suit Bill, because he had never been one to enjoy a deep contentment. The environmentalist was actively opposed to the Cold War, nuclear weapons, the Vietnam War, and fascism. Time and again, he opened his home to people who were politically persecuted, which is why the Swiss Federal Intelligence Service kept such a close eye on him for 25 years. In the end, the kitchen clock was just the beginning of a series of chronographic successes: In 1961, Junghans finally incorporated its clear but special dial into a wristwatch that was just as purist and which stood out from the increasingly pretentious watches of the era precisely because it did not take part in the arms race. The watch has long since been listed as an art piece in the design collection of the Museum of Modern Art in New York.

A beautiful gift, without ostentation, in all modesty. As a reconciliation gift, you could also have the numeral 4 represent whatever you like: 4 you. Or in reference to the similarity with an overturned chair: You knock me off my seat.

Flemming Lassen | 1935

The Tired Man

White, fluffy, and rather clumsy. At first glance, polar bears look perfectly cuddly. The two fur balls named Knut and Flocke, born in 2006 and 2007, attracted record numbers of visitors to the Berlin and Nuremberg zoos. Since 2018, the climate crisis has turned the image of a polar bear on an ice floe into something practically iconic. Indeed, upholstered furniture companies seem to have fallen asleep at the wheel. After all, they could have easily championed the furry beast. The designers have in fact always viewed its cuddle factor as something worth emulating. Francesco Binfaré, for instance, designed Pack, a sofa in the shape of a prostrate polar bear, while Flemming Lassen of Denmark compared the comfort of his famous Tired Man armchair with the pleasure a baby polar bear derives from lying in the arms of its mother. He probably no longer had *Brehm's Animal Life* to hand, but he might have suspected that polar bears are not that into pleasant warmth. The animals can easily tolerate temperatures as low as minus 45 Celsius, and instead of resting comfortably in their mothers' fur, they cling to it firmly with sharp claws. While they're at it, the little tykes must watch out that their uncles or neighbors don't make a meal of them, since male polar bears will not shy away from the most ruthless tactics to make their mates ready for copulation. It was therefore a clever move to avoid comparisons with cuddly animals and give the chair a name that evokes a differed image: Tired Man.

The Tired Man armchair radiates pure comfort—an invitation to all weary people.

Lassen's purpose in building his many fluffy prototypes was always to create a warm and soft environment, to make the world fluffier and rest periods more stylish. The armchair envelops us in powerful arms. The Tired Man of 1935 is an honest-to-goodness, large-format wingback chair. But Ingeborg, another chair he designed five years later, was massively solid. Both chairs are upholstered in cuddly sheepskin and are love tokens to that unique feeling of sitting in the comfort of one's own home. Incidentally, the teenage Flemming Lassen and his brother Mogens were schoolmates with the great Arne Jacobsen, and Jacobsen was the one who convinced his buddy to take up architecture instead of painting. In 1929, Flemming and Arne were following the same career path, and they designed the house of the future for a competition. It was a round structure with flat screen televisions hanging on the walls and a helipad on the roof. A rather low-key version of the high-tech lifestyle that the two men envisioned. In the uncertain times that followed, Europe's political atmosphere grew more tense, and a armchair can sometimes have a diffusing effect. In such a world, a Tired Man understands that sometimes all you want to do is hole up somewhere and seek refuge in a comfortable hideaway; Ingeborg then also made you feel as though you were sheltered in the loving arms of your mother. But let's face it, that's just kitchen sink psychology. The chair was nevertheless manufactured for just a few years, only to disappear into obscurity. But its value as a rare object naturally raised its price for connoisseurs. After being auctioned in 2014, the original Tired Man has become the most expensive chair ever sold in Denmark, where it went for a cool 200,000 euros. For the same price, you could by a whole house elsewhere.

But let's get back to the polar bears. Perhaps they indeed have more to do with our armchair that it seemed at first. The animals are asleep a good two-thirds of the day. And the Tired Man knows exactly how that feels.

Sitting in the Tired Man you should feel like a polar bear cub snuggling up to its mother—that was Flemming Lassen's idea.

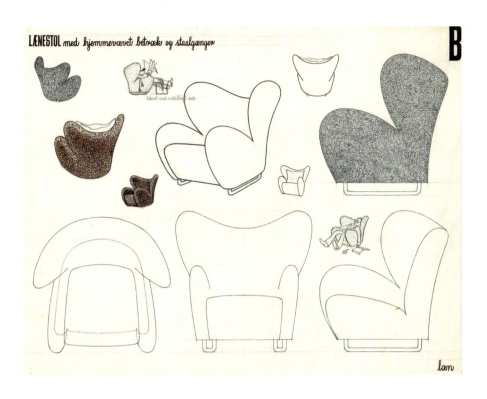

FAILURE OR NOT?
This rather small "cooking box" never became the housewife's best friend.

There are a lot of magical places on Earth where love originates, where decisions are made that change the world, where events are celebrated and life lessons are learned, where people argue and dishes are smashed. Sometimes all these places are wrapped into one: the kitchen. We fill our other rooms with life but the kitchen has a life of its own, it seems to have its own pulse, it's the heart of our home. It's where we prepare spaghetti or a thick steak as well as forge policies and make plans. For eons it remained humbly in the background, gradually evolving from the hearth, to the sooty open-hearth kitchen slightly separated from the living area, to a design piece that forms the center of our homes. But in every decade, in every century, the kitchen has been training our taste buds and our senses in the art of enjoying food. Spices imported from around the world refined our tastes. The first cookbooks appeared in the 16th century. Did they have temperature control in those days? Of course! You just had to raise or lower the pot that was suspended from a tripod over the fire.

Margarete Schütte-Lihotzky | 1926

Frankfurt Kitchen

Meanwhile, the zeitgeist was following its own course and making fine adjustments to the kitchen's evolution. Whereas people in rural areas would never have surrendered their eat-in kitchens where three or four generations could assemble around the table, city dwellers soon devised an alternative design that accommodated their increasingly frantic lifestyle and shrinking per-capita living space. It was no longer about coziness. It was about fewer steps between appliances. In 1912, American home economist Christine Frederick used a stopwatch to measure how long it took to rinse lettuce, chop vegetables, do the dishes, and perform other similar tasks. Optimization of the housewife's sphere of activity had arrived. In 1927, a thousand subsidized dwellings were built in Frankfurt as part of a new urban planning measure, with kitchens designed by the 30-year-old Viennese architect Margarete Schütte-Lihotzky. These kitchens were ergonomic, practical, and followed a sophisticated design. Until then, kitchens had tended to be crammed with standalone pieces of furniture—a cabinet here, a sink there.

Could have been a milestone in terms of equality: The idea was that women should not spend so much time in the kitchen but be able to do other things instead.

Kitchen

But the brand-new Frankfurt kitchen was all of a piece. Their cabinet fronts were painted a fine blue, not so much to conform to contemporary tastes as to deter unwanted visitors: The color supposedly repelled flies. Integrated storage bins, pull-out work surfaces, a sort of trapdoor in the counter for disposing of waste, and a fold-out ironing board and table mounted on the wall were all contained with a space hardly bigger than 6.5 square meters. Everything was so compact and flat that it could all be cleaned with a single swipe of a dishcloth. Consisting only of wood and metal, the materials were already sustainable at a time when hardly anyone saw this as an asset. The price of a kitchen plunged from 500 marks to half that amount, thanks to mass production. But German housewives were never reconciled to it. Was it too avant-garde? Who knows? Feminists saw the mini-kitchen as a kind of women's prison cell.

People learn by trial and error. The kitchen has long been transformed from its role as a mere workplace to a place of enjoyment that's bursting with life. There's a reason why parties always end up in the kitchen. It's a place of endless possibilities.

Pull-out additional table (bottom), labeled chutes (left side): Margarete Schütte-Lihotzky's thoroughly thought out and practically designed kitchen

The Frankfurt kitchen from 1926 is considered the world's first built-in kitchen.

Gatti, Paolini and Teodoro | 1968
Sacco

Even piece of furniture has a family tree with antecedents and a story that is always interwoven with history itself. So any pouffe or oversized floor cushion that believes itself to be the epitome of a new, casual sitting culture should get over itself and engage in a bit of genealogical research. After all, its great-grandparents were sewn from camel leather or lambskin and lay about on the floors of nomad tents in the lands of the Maghreb centuries ago. At the turn of the twentieth century, they even made their way to French Belle Époque society, where they turned up in the novels of Marcel Proust and Emile Zola and furnished many a fictional living room. Lounging about in comfort was therefore nothing new, although people had pushed this idea aside for many decades until the flower children called for revolution in the 1960s. 1968 was a turbulent year. War in Vietnam, the Khmer Rouge's rein of terror in Cambodia, military rule in Greece, Martin Luther King shot to death in Memphis, street battles raging in France. Young people staged revolts. Against politicians, the ruling class, and even against their parents, who refused to abandon long-held beliefs. The younger generation declared their obedience to rebellion. They waged their own war on narrow-mindedness, conventions, and strict formality. They wanted to blur boundaries and make them permeable. They preferred a soft touch to rigidity. The first piece of furniture to embrace the zeitgeist was the Blow armchair by De Pas, D'Urbino, and Lomazzi (▶ p. 218). Inflatable and lacking firm lines, it nevertheless had a definable shape, strictly speaking. Three other Italians decided to take this concept one step further and came up with a chair that took on the very shape of its owner, making it exceedingly deformable. Piero Gatti, Cesare Paolini, and Franco Teodoro invented Sacco, the mother of all beanbags. They began with a couple of sketches,

91

and the rest involved a whole lot of trial and error. The designers filled a PVC shell first with water, then leaves, feathers, lead beads, and ping-pong balls. Only when they experimented with Styrofoam beads did they find the perfect solution for a kind of seat that offered comfort instead of demanding a certain posture. A chair you could really sink into. The three designers' mothers sewed the prototypes at home. The photo of one specimen somehow landed in a newspaper, where it came to the attention of the head of purchasing at Macy's department store in New York. He immediately reached for the phone and ordered ten thousand units from the three young men. Overwhelmed, and perhaps even blindsided, they knocked on Aurelio Zanotta's door and asked him to produce the Saccos.

The rest is history. And the beanbag has long since aged into an old geezer. But one who can keep up with the times. On Sacco's 50th birthday, Zanotta issued a special edition with a green image: organic polyester beads made from sugar cane and a cover from recycled plastic and old fishing nets. After all, adaptability has always been deeply embedded in its DNA.

Max Bill | 1954
Ulm Stool

You might think that furniture tends to stay out of world events. It stands around and makes the odd aesthetic statement, and in doing so reaches the limits of its core expertise. Not so fast. Interior design and the way a society thinks are very closely entwined. Indeed, Scandinavia is often viewed as a kind of neutral terrain, one in which nature has the upper hand when it comes to style. But in taking this view, we could not be more wrong. The Danes, for instance, understood perfectly that beauty should be accessible to all. No Danish citizen would willingly make any attempt to stand out from the crowd, and they even prefer to share all the conveniences their country has to offer than to turn them into exclusive goods reserved for the few. There are historical reasons for this, and it also goes back to the legacy of the1950s democrats: politics, in fact.

Danish modern, a style that captivated the design world at the time, emerged from this very mind-set. Plain and without frills, stripped down to the essentials, functional, and fit for mass consumption. The great creatives, from Arne Jacobsen and Kay Bojesen to Verner Panton and Louis Poulsen, always created designs for everyone. Take the famous Jacobsen "7," for instance, a laminated wood chair originally intended for a company cafeteria. And this idea also resonated in other countries. In America, Charles and Ray Eames tinkered with the democratic design style that everyone could afford, and in postwar Germany, many ideas thrived that were intended to make life more pleasant across all social strata.

The Ulm School of Design was especially active in this area, and one of its teachers was the architect Max Bill. True to his credo of making everyday design affordable to everyone as well as socially and politically responsible, he created not only furniture, but also bathtubs, electrical plugs, clothes hangers, hairbrushes, and other objects. Bill firmly believed that beauty made the world better, more humane. However, he also felt that nothing was truly beautiful unless it was also practical and free of bells and whistles. And so he designed the Ulm footstool in 1954, a joint effort with Dutch architect Hans Gugelot, the master cabinetmaker Paul Hildinger, and Bill's own students. Three boards and a sort of broom handle: that's all there was to the modest seat, which was built in the university workshop from donated wood. But the footstool is also a jack of all trades. You can sit on it, use it as a side table, a tray, shelf, and even as a conveyance. All these modalities went into its job description, when dozens of these footstools made their way into the Ulm School. It is a first-rate democrat, the best proof that design can indeed be political. And also evidence of a surprising conclusion: politics can indeed be this beautiful.

92

A simple, robust piece of wooden furniture that can be used in many ways: the Ulm stool.

Jasper Morrison | 2013

Pirandello

Writing desks are traitors. They betray secrets with abandon and are often as revealing as the contents of a woman's handbag or the space around a bathroom sink. Is the owner a slob or an accomplished organizer? A self-promoter or a contender for a medal in humility? Flip through *Über Schreibtische* (About Desks), a book containing collected photos of famous desk jockeys by Konrad Rufus Müller and Sten Nadolny, and you will quickly reach this conclusion: size really does matter. And from time to time, so does megalomania. Mitterrand in the Elysée Palace. Attention-seeking Putin, who placed his center of power in an enormous office. Helmut Kohl's office manager offers an interesting glimpse of life on the periphery of power with dozens of china elephants arranged on the edges of her desk. Or West German Chancellor Helmut Schmidt, who occasionally attended to his correspondence in the lounge car of a special train during his 1980 election campaign. While waiting for the photographer to arrive, Frank-Walter Steinmeier, the former German Minister of Foreign Affairs, was evidently thinking of Albert Einstein's apt remark: "If a cluttered desk is a sign of a cluttered mind, what, then, does an empty desk suggest about its user?" Steinmeier admitted to having brought in a few stacks of files for his photo, saying that they made him look more important. And yet a good piece of the world was governed from these few square inches of space—picture that. Or worlds were built there. Most poets don't write in bed, as did Albert Dürer's "Poor Poet." They tend to work on writing surfaces with or without an underframe. Luigi Pirandello, the Nobel Laureate in Literature, sometimes wrote at a kind of secretary and sometimes at an oversized desk, as documented by various photos from the time. We'll leave aside for the moment the fact that he was born in a neighborhood of Agrigento, Sicily, known as Càvusu—which roughly translates from Italian as chaos—and we will definitely not draw any conclusions from this name. The man was a genius. Even if he did sometimes do strange things, like the time he had his Nobel Prize medal melted down to help fund Mussolini's military campaign in Abyssinia. At the very least, Pirandello was familiar with the desperate battle for words and stories. Indeed, the idea for his famous play titled *Six Characters in Search of an Author* derived from this struggle.

However, Pirandello evidently inspired another master in a different discipline to come up with his own stroke of genius. Designer Jasper Morrison created a special desk and named it after the Italian writer. A piece of furniture made of glass with a wooden footrest. A highly minimalist design and completely see-through. A desk that not only famous authors but also other desk jockeys could certainly love to call their own.

246　Outdoor furniture

Erwan and Ronan Bouroullec | 2015

Palissade

Sometimes success is a family affair. There are plenty of siblings who've achieved international fame in the same discipline: the American directors and screenwriters Joel and Ethan Coen, who made film history with *Fargo* and their multiple-Oscar-winning *No Country for Old Men*, tennis player sisters Venus and Serena Williams, the three Bee Gee brothers, and boxers Vitali and Vladimir Klitschko. A double act in sports is a little harder to pull off, but at some point the Coen brothers and the Bee Gees decided to merge their talents with fantastic results.

In the case of Erwan and Ronan Bouroullec, it initially seemed like their interests pulled them in different directions. As kids, they fought like cats and dogs and as teenagers, they preferred to avoid each other completely. Erwan wanted to be an artist, he loved Indie music bands and dreamed of a life of complete freedom. His brother Ronan, on the other hand, was already fascinated by the world of objects at age 15. One wanted to shape his environment while the other wanted to run riot in it, and yet the two philosophies ultimately did manage to converge. Immediately after Ronan finished his design degree in 1996, he opened his own studio and Erwan, who was still in school, worked for him as an assistant. The two received their first joint commission from design boss Giulio Cappellini when they presented a kitchen at the 1998 Milan Furniture Fair. Since then, the brothers have become France's most well-known design exports, their differences are history, and they jet through the interior design world on a single wavelength.

As teenagers they argued, as designers they harmonize: the Bouroullec brothers.

All their designs undergo a rite of passage. Each one has to pass the ultimate test in the brothers' garage in Provence, against the backdrop of a priceless view of the surrounding landscape. A good piece has to stand on its own without sacrificing grandeur. It's a reality check that demonstrates a higher insight: Interior design isn't just a matter of placing different objects and conditions side by side, nor is it a boxing match between them. The goal is a draw, not a knockout.

In the case of their Palissade bench for the Danish label Hay, the brothers knew immediately that it would pass the test. It had what it took to be a star—in cities, on terraces, in front of bars, or in parks. In terms of materials, the Bouroullecs briefly played with the idea that aluminum might be classier than powder-coated steel, until they realized that a light weight could have heavy consequences. A safe and secure bench is worth more than a bench that takes flight in a high wind. Once the Bouroullecs have finished designing an object and it has passed the acid test in Provence, Ronan photographs it. This lets him take a step back and look at it more objectively, he once said. And if the newbie fails the photo shoot? Maybe the Bouroullecs employ the same dreaded phrase that's so familiar to fans of Germany's Next Top Model: "Unfortunately, I have no photo for you today." The Palissade bench did, of course, escape this fate.

Made of hard steel, but radiating coziness.
And above all chic.

Hella Jongerius | 2015

Polder

When things get stuck or stagnate in the flow of thoughts, coaches, therapists or management consultants like to advise a change of perspective. So you simply look at things from a different angle, approach them from the side, from the front or from behind. You get particularly nice insights if you simply rise above everything, look down from above, or even stand above things: seen from a bird's eye view, the big picture becomes visible, and even huge obstacles suddenly seem rather puny. Sometimes it's only then that you understand how things are connected.

In his work of the century, the photographer Yann Artus Bertrand provided dreamlike aerial photographs from all over the world, in which one thing above all can be recognized: the earth is beautiful. Bertrand also flew over the Netherlands on his

95

mission, above the tulip fields near Amsterdam, which from above look like a colorful graphic work of art. Only the polder meadows he apparently overlooked: The patches of land that man wrestled from the sea by building dikes. They lie like puzzle pieces in front of the North Sea, crisscrossed by canals, small lakes, and canals. Somehow a miracle, but in any case beautiful. It was precisely these green spaces of her homeland that Dutch designer Hella Jongerius memorialized in 2015 with the asymmetrical cushions of her famous Polder sofa, colored in different shades of a basic tone. Yet you don't even need a change of perspective to see at a glance the kinship with the Dutch lands: At least in the green version, the cushions lie side by side like fields of different sizes. Short or long, with a lot of offset and in complete disregard of the fact that seat and back cushions on sofas usually agree on the same width.

Hella, whose real first name is Wilhelmina Maria Cornelia—too pretty to be left unmentioned—had to be persuaded with angels' tongues to design a sofa in the first place. The woman who, incidentally, also designed the KLM cabin interior and was the first woman ever to be named Designer of the Year at the Salon du Meuble in Paris in 2004, doesn't like Sofas at all. The Polder upholstery has nevertheless turned out very well for her, and the source of inspiration has also rubbed off on it in a completely different way: The fields were wrestled from the sea, and even for the place on the sofa one will have to fight for. Because the person sitting on it at the moment won't leave it voluntarily anytime soon.

You really can't go wrong with a combination of blue and white. Certainly not when it comes to furnishing a vacation home, though you really should restrain yourself somewhat when it comes to making maritime style statements. Regardless, blue and white have always proven to be a patented dream team in terms of aesthetics. Bavarians proudly display the two colors on their flag, and during the rococo period, blue painters emerged who decorated entire rooms using blue and white as a color combination. Some kind of blue-and-white tableware is much more universal and can be found in a surprisingly large number of households. And that, too, has a long history. We begin our search for clues in China—the country we like to turn up our noses at because we suspect, not entirely without reason, that artistry in the Middle Kingdom has now become strongly oriented towards the discipline of making perfect reproductions. It's a shame, actually, and partly undeserved, because for thousands of years the Chinese played a pioneering role in arts and crafts—and thus also in the beautification of the environment. The ancestors of our most beautiful blue-and-white tableware, for example, came from the Far East, or more precisely from the city of Jingdezhen, China. There, more than 800 years ago, artisans started applying cobalt paint under the glaze to create lovely blue patterns on the previously somewhat dull white vases and plates. The shade looked pretty, never too busy, pleasantly restrained on the plain porcelain pieces, and lasted an astonishingly long time. The West was burning with envy, but the Chinese would not give up their color secret. In times of need, people made do with crude copies. In the 17th century, people coated earthenware with a white tin glaze and used their own techniques to transform them into blue-and-white porcelain pieces, imitating the entire world of Chinese patterns on their plates and vases. As a consequence, exotic flowers blossomed, dragons coiled, and birds flapped their wings. Only slowly did domestic plants begin to appear in the decorations, and the famous and almost ubiquitous strawflower and bulb patterns emerged.

Hedwig Bollhagen | 1955

Tableware 137

The blue stripes with which ceramist Hedwig Bollhagen painted her tableware, on the other hand, seem almost clumsy in comparison with the engraved Chinese decorations, and the potbellied shapes of her pieces seem cottage-like in the best sense of the word. But in their simplicity they blended beautifully with the Bauhaus style.

Born in Hanover, Bollhagen designed her everyday dishes in 1955 in Marwitz near Berlin. Her intention was "not to make fashionable hits, but rather simple, timeless things." The fact that her work was suddenly considered art rather irritated her: "Oh yes, some people call it that. I make plates, cups, and jugs," she said, waving it off. "They're just pots!" she commented more than once. However, her work garnered numerous international accolades and was even recognized as state art by the rather unsubtle GDR. Following the forced merger of Bollhagen's HB-Werkstätten für Keramik with the VEB Steingutwerk, after the fall of the Berlin Wall she was finally able to reprivatize her workshop in 1993. Even at the age of 90, she would still open the door every morning. Clad in her blue-and-white smock, she would walk through the rows of her painters, checking that the lines on the pots were perfectly in place. It is easy to imagine that Hedwig has long since been floating on some cloud high above the HB-Werkstätten. On a white cloud in a blue sky.

Christian Werner | 2015
2002

Some things simply catch on from the very start. The world welcomes them with open arms and places them on a pedestal. Things that delight us from the first moment we see them and cause us to stare in wonder. Some people, of course, simply itch to repeat the experience once again later on. There are plenty of examples these days. The celebrated 1960 film, *Purple Noon*, was remade as *The Talented Mr. Ripley*, which garnered four Oscar nominations in 1999. Francis Ford Coppola's *The Great Gatsby*, which starred Robert Redford in 1974, met its match in the new version from 2013 with Leonardo DiCaprio in the leading role. Sometimes the remake even outdoes the original. The old Beatles song, "With a Little Help From My Friends", never enjoyed the success of the cover sung by Joe Cocker.

Still, yesterday's stars have a hard time filling stadiums on the strength of their top hits decades after they made it big. And yet the Simple Minds and Chris Norman still go on tour with their golden oldies from the 1970s and 1980s. You might tear up at the sight of these senior troubadours on their concert posters, looking just as fresh as in the glory days of their youth. They seem to be denied the right to age gracefully. On the other hand, when the superstar pop group Abba rose from the ashes in 2021, they didn't merely rest on their earlier laurels, but confidently relaunched themselves with new songs in their old style. When it comes to interior design, there are similar ways to deal with classic models of success. Re-editions are usually the way to go. Old wine in new wineskins, so to speak. An icon is given a new color, perhaps one detail is altered. Everything else remains the same.

However, to render a completely new and entirely modern interpretation of a classic is a risky business. And so when the brothers Peter and Philipp Thonet, CEOs of a tradition-rich company in Frankenberg, nimbly took not just a small step but a giant leap into the future, the move took everyone by surprise. The pièce de résistance that had once made the family-run enterprise famous was the renowned coffee shop chair made from bentwood, created by their grandfather Michael Thonet in 1859. The second icon was Chair 209, more or less updated from the 1920s version. It found its way into almost all model homes designed by the best architects: in Le Corbusier's Pavillon de L'Esprit Nouveau de Paris, in Villa de la Rocha, Maisons La Roche et Jeanneret in Paris, and in Mart Stam's row houses in the Stuttgart Weißenhof development. Le Corbusier rhapsodized on the "nobility" of the design; his Danish colleague, Poul Henningsen, found it to be perfect.

Indeed, the chair made from bent laminated wood had sold in the millions worldwide as early as the Bauhaus era, not least because it was easy to ship en masse. A crate measuring one cubic meter could hold 36 units, each one tidily disassembled into six pieces, which had to be screwed together upon reaching their final destination. In short, the chair was nearly perfect, and there was nothing more to add to the bent wood story.

Nevertheless, the two brothers invited the designer Christian Werner to join them at their trade show booth and asked whether he wouldn't like to design a couch made of bent wood. Werner was "immediately all fired up," and "I though it was a marvelous idea!" And so he sketched a two seater "with classic pen and paper," whose removable cushions rested on two elegant bent wood frames. To be completely certain that the design would actually work, he immediately built a prototype. The Thonet brothers were delighted, as was their head of marketing. It was the first time he'd ever been able get comfortable with the first draft of a design. However, such a lovely piece really deserves a better name than "2002." At first glance, the number might lead you to think it refers to the sofa's birth year. But who is willing to admit to being older than their actual age? The sofa was designed in 2015. A bright young thing with illustrious antecedents. The scion of a good family, whose beauty doesn't come only from its genes but also springs from a brand new idea. At the instigation of two brothers who dared to reinvent the wheel. Kudos to them!

Daring and winning: With the „2002" bentwood sofa, Christian Werner designed a characterful new interpretation for the traditional house of Thonet.

Michael Schneider | 1995
Mono Zeug

Once upon a time there was a German town called Mettmann. And if you think you can't expect any fabulous stories from there, you are very much mistaken. Apart from the fact that hikers describe the wild Neandertal Valley near the small Rhineland town as magical, the famous Neanderthal swung his club there around the Ice Age. And this is precisely what led to the design of perhaps one of the most innovative cutlery sets in the world.

In 1989, the habits of the prehistoric man roaming through the undergrowth inspired Michael Schneider, then a design student, to write a required term paper for Stuttgart professor Richard Sapper: the task was to design an object consisting of several parts that only made sense together. The assignment caught Schneider in a kind of rebellious phase in which he questioned everything and wanted to radically change the world of design. For example, he found it completely pointless that a complete set of cutlery was always laid out in the same way, even though the fork, spoon or knife had completely different functions. Go back to the roots, the young designer thought, and remembered the Neanderthal man: who cut with a hand axe, scooped water in the hollow of his hand, picked something with a skewer and stirred it with his finger. His design for a completely new type of cutlery first landed on his professor's desk, then in a competition, and finally with Wilhelm Seibel senior, then head of the cutlery manufacturer Mono in Mettmann. His company had always focused on things that were a stone's throw ahead of the times: When the love of old German period furniture was still flourishing in local living rooms, this Company from small town Mettmann sent the radically simple Mono A cutlery by design professor Peter Raacke into the race. It sold lousily until the country finally cleared the air for modernism in the 1970s, when the slender design won one prize after another and even graced the 110-stamp in 1999.

In its outrageousness, Mono Zeug wrote a piece of history without following a time-honored tradition. It literally cut through old habits, picked out the most important characteristics of cutlery, and drew on the full range of creativity. Designer Michael Schneider miraculously combined quite a number of stories: that of the small town in the Neandertal Valley and its most famous inhabitant, that of the Mono company and its cutlery culture. Four parts forming one big whole. Once upon a time in Mettmann. There you go!

Corradino D'Ascanio had designed war planes, and after 1945 he actually hated motorcycles and wanted to build helicopters. The man was clearly drawn to higher things when, a year after the end of the war, Enrico Piaggio commissioned him to design a motorized two-wheeler. It was by no means a prestige project. In the USA, people had been riding around on mopeds since the 1920s, and Piaggio had already come up with a template of sorts in the form of a motorscooter christened "Paperino" (as the Italians called Donald Duck), but it had simply not impressed the boss. D'Ascanio's version would eventually change the world and, above all, make it a little more beautiful. When Piaggio saw the design, he exclaimed, "It looks like a wasp!" and the scooter was named accordingly: Vespa.

The Vespa not only came along at the right time, it came from the right place as well. Soon after the war, Italy became a place of longing, where lemons and oranges hung from the trees and the air held the wonderful promise of warmth and sunshine. On the Vespa, you could ride towards freedom, lightness and, above all, better days. Its contours seemed to represent the momentum with which things were destined to look up. The technology was well concealed in the scooter, which took just 21.4 seconds to cover a kilometer in the record-breaking year of 1951. This meant that people always had their eyes on what mattered most: the style, the importance that Italians attached to *fare bella figura* (making a good impression), and the certainty that they would always look good on it. Advertising immediately got on board the snazzy bench seat: "Vespizzatevi" or "Let's Vespa!" was the slogan of the 1950s campaign, but the fact that Audrey Hepburn and Gregory Peck rolled through Rome on it in *Roman Holiday* is probably what drove sales figures much higher.

Corradino D'Ascanio | 1946

Vespa

Much like the Apple computer decades later, the Vespa was a machine that became a beloved object of desire. Because it epitomized a lifestyle, dressed in the colors of fashion, and adorned itself with the trappings of beauty, the scooter made it into countless advertising campaigns for new fragrances and clothes, ranging from Agent Provocateur, Donna Karan, and Dolce & Gabbana to Vivienne Westwood and Christian Dior. At a store in Paris, fashion designer Yves Saint Laurent even unveiled his own unique version—a matte black lacquer-and-leather beauty with high-gloss accents and a handmade leather saddle. But what's fascinating is how the scooter has confidently navigated its way through all the various fashions without adapting its silhouette to the zeitgeist in any significant way. This is where past, present, and future all travel through the world together. Only a true classic can do that.

And even if D'Ascanio no longer designed helicopters, he still good reason to take flight. Especially given that his invention has provided around 18 million people with the most stylish ride since 1946.

FAILURE OR NOT?
The Fleeze can do just about anything, but it does not go with every interior style.

There's a surprising number of people who are so successful in two disciplines that they're able turn both into careers. In recent years, while scrolling through Instagram and leafing through various colorful celebrity magazines, I've been struck by the dominance of certain combinations. The world seems to be full of models who design jewelry or bikinis on the side and/or act and/or conquer the market as influencers. And more power to them—especially since most of these women must have real natural talent, because their activities certainly aren't based on serious training. But from an orthopedic surgeon, we can expect genuine expertise that's in no way related to that of a designer—not even remotely. Nevertheless, there's a certain logic in the fact that Winfried Totzek, a physician who works with bones, suddenly decided to design a lounge chair. The man whose patients were constantly complaining of back trouble was a simple practitioner who understood only too well the consequences of inferior beds and chairs. He himself never sat still, his body was always moving, and he couldn't stand chairs that locked him into a fixed position. Putting his feet up on the windowsill, rocking back and forth in a rocker, and constantly changing his position came much more naturally. Because he had no piece of furniture that supported his style, he decided to invent one: the Fleeze. The name is derived from the somewhat slangy and profoundly German word "fläzen," meaning to lounge or sprawl. That says it all. The lounger's head and foot sections are fully adjustable, allowing you to sprawl, stretch out, or lie almost head over heels. He entrusted its manufacture to a maker of orthopedic shoes who produced it according to Totzek's plans. "The prototype," Totzek recalled, "looked a little clumsy." It took several versions before he was satisfied with the results and started shopping his adjustable marvel around to several manufacturers. Most of them wearily declined.

Winfried Totzek | 1988

Fleeze

Intended exactly as the name "Fleeze" implies, the small retro-style sofa was made for uninhibited lounging.

Too many physicians had already offered them too many designs, none of which were any good. But the Swiss upholstered furniture manufacturer de Sede showed an interest—and Totzek showed his pig-headedness during the negotiations. The Swiss company's lawyer was shaking his head at Totzek's financial demands when, at exactly 11:10 p.m., the orthopedist announced that he would sit at the piano and remain there until 12:00, at which time he would go home with or without a contract. Totzek played evergreens non-stop until just before midnight when the lawyer finally tapped him on the shoulder and said, "We'll do it."

The Fleeze debuted in 1988 at the Cologne Furniture Fair, where it was so idolized that the de Sede team called Totzek's office and ordered the master to come to Cologne immediately. Totzek recalled only two times in his professional career when he sent patients home: when his dog died and that day for the Fleeze.

Visible softness, volume, comfort: Ron Arad thought of the Big Easy Chair as a lushly upholstered club chair.

Ron Arad | 1988

Big Easy Chair

The world has always situated genius and madness in close proximity to each other, but sometimes even the most mundane of stimulants can help to spur creativity. Montmartre painter Henri de Toulouse-Lautrec was addicted to absinthe (which is why one variety is named after him), author Robert Louis Stevenson allegedly wrote *Dr. Jekyll and Mr. Hyde* under the influence of cocaine in just six days, and even J.R.R. Tolkien is also said to have used drugs to fuel his imagination for *The Lord of the Rings*. And quite honestly, in furniture design, too, there are concepts that might make the interested observer wonder just what on earth the designer was smoking when this thing came into being?

Ron Arad's Big Easy Chair, for example, actually looks as if it came straight out of the White Rabbit's household furnishings in *Alice in Wonderland*. And as an interesting sidenote, the author of this classic, Lewis Carroll, is also said to have used psychedelics while writing. Arad was in fact completely in command of his senses when he created the voluminous single-seater; he had been thinking of a club chair that had been so lavishly overstuffed that it was bursting at the seams. But most of all, he seemed to have been driven by the sheer desire to practice a new skill he had just learned—that of welding. "I could bend it, cut it, weld it, fold it, torture the piece of metal until it made a comfortable chair," he explained enthusiastically. Sometimes even the most hardened of people buckle under brutal torture methods, but in this case these methods served a really good purpose—the creation of a masterpiece.

Arad had always been considered a punk figure in the design scene, dating back to the early 1980s when he experimented with ever-new and often raw materials with visible welds that he splashed wildly with paint... And why, pray tell, should anything have changed? After his first bare steel armchairs, he took pity on those who preferred softer surfaces, and he covered them with upholstery and red leather. Another time he polished the steel to a mirror finish, while the time after that he turned the basic shape into a shining piece composed of steel spheres. In 1991, he graciously gave in to the request from furniture goddess Patrizia Moroso and entrusted the Big Easy to her for mass production. From that point on, it was available in leather and finally in colored polyethylene. One unique piece, which he had painted like a work of art, fetched almost $200,000 at auction in 2008. And Ron Arad is far from finished with the Big Easy. During the COVID-19 lockdown, he was already at it again, giving his classic a makeover. "Somehow," says Arad, "the Big Easy has always survived."

INDEX

1 2 3
2002 254

A
Aalto, Aino 17, 195
Aalto, Alvar 17, 195
Aarnio, Eero 69, 220
Aarnio, Pirkko 69
AB 1 Alarm Clock 51
Abba 254
Acapulco Chair 58
Action Office Desk 128
Adenauer, Konrad 91
Adler, Jonathan 210
Agent Provocateur 259
Air 99
Albers, Josef 227
Alessi 82, 123, 192
Alessi, Alberto 82, 123, 192
Alkalay, Shay 92
Altorfer AG 81
Altorfer deck chair 81
Altorfer jr., Huldreich 81
American Airlines 153
Anderberg, Rolf 36
Andrews, Julie 69
Andriot, Chantal 29
Antelope Chair 209
Antibodi 157
Apple 204, 259
Apple iMac 204
Arad, Ron 201, 265
Araignée 71
Arco 87
Arens, Egmont H. 135
Arita 141
Armstrong-Jones, Antony,
 Earl of Snowdon 218
Artichoke 125
Aubecq, Octave 143
Audrito, Franco 65
Auma factory 61
Avedon, Richard 65
Axelsson, Ake 36

B
B3 Club Chair 144
B 9 144
Badovici, Jean 154
Baijings, Carole 92
Ball Chair 69
Ball Clock 10
Banksy 36
Barcelona Chair 111, 220
Barneys 210
Bauer, Reinhold 99
Bauhaus 24, 51, 61, 77, 111, 144, 154, 176, 184,
 202, 205, 218, 222, 227, 231, 253, 255
Bayer, Otto 148
Beatles 254
Becher, Bernd 45
Becher, Hilla 45
Beckenbauer, Franz 196
Becker, Dorothee 137
Bee Gees 247
Bergman, Ingrid 18
Berlusconi, Silvio 66
Bertrand, Yann Artus 250
Besau, Marcel 92
Beuys, Joseph 91
Beyoncé 65
Bierut, Michael 153
Big Easy Chair 265
Bill, Max 214, 231, 242
Billy 121
Binfaré, Francesco 233
Blahnik, Manolo 218
Bloomingdale's 153
Blow 43, 99, 218
Bocca 63
Bojesen, Kay 36, 47, 184, 242
Bolle 66
Bollhagen, Hedwig 253
Bonnier publishing house 109
Bookworm 201
Bouroullec, Erwan 247
Bouroullec, Ronan 247
Branson, Richard 24
Brassau, Pierre 36
Braun 51, 130
Breuer, Marcel 144, 225, 227
Brio 138
Brno Chair 112
Brunner, Klaus 117
Bulb 52
Burton, Richard 231
Butterfly 213
Butterfly Chair 87
by Lassen 79

C
Cabbage Chair 15
Cappellini, Giulio 247
Carl Hansen & Søn 41
Carroll, Lewis 265
Carter, Jimmy 190
Casati, Luisa 96
Cassina 203
Castelli Ferrieri, Anna 12
Castiglioni, Achille 87
Castiglioni, Pier Giacomo 87
Catherine, Duchess of Cambridge 231
Cavalieri, Lina 96
Centre Georges-Pompidou 29, 201
Chair 209 255
Chanel 55, 161
Chanel, Coco 55, 77, 157
Christensen, Birger 79
Christian Dior 259
Claesson Koivisto Rune 229
Claesson, Mårten 229
Clooney, George 143
Cochrane, Josephine M. 132
Cocker, Joe 254
Coen, Ethan 247
Coen, Joel 247
Coffee Table 161
Colomina, Beatriz 216
Componibili 12
Connery, Sean 196
Continental 176
Coppola, Francis Ford 254
Cor 216
Craig, Daniel 12
Craven Walker, Edward 31
Cylinda-line 56

D
Dahl, Birger 190
Dahl, Gary 206
Dalí, Gala 65
Dalí, Salvador 41, 63, 192
Daniel, Bob 107
Danmark design museum 17
D'Ascanio, Corradino 259
Day-Lewis, Daniel 182
Dell, Christian 61
Delon, Alain 254
de Lucchi, Michele 176
Depardieu, Gérard 71

De Pas, Jonathan 43, 99, 219
de Piles, Roger 227
Desaegher, Armand 143
de Sede 263
Design Letters 206
DiCaprio, Leonardo 69, 254
Diez, Stefan 141
Dixon, Tom 31
Djinn Chair 128
Dokka 190
Dolce & Gabbana 259
Donna Karan 259
Dreher, Peter 125
D'Urbino, Donato 43, 99, 218, 219, 240

E
E1 Desk 114
E 1027 154
Eames, Charles 92, 95, 111, 119, 163, 242
Eames, Lucia 164
Eames, Ray 92, 95, 111, 119, 163, 242
Eco, Umberto 123
Egelund, Kasper 171
Egg Chair 196, 206
Eiermann, Egon 114, 117
Einstein, Albert 245
Eisenbrand, Jochen 10
Elephant 163, 220
Elfa 109
EM77 55
Embru 81
Engman, Marcus 99
Eternit 21

F
Fabricius, Preben 183
Falk, Alexander 81
Fermob 77
Ferrari 88
Ferrari, Enea 220
Fischer, Curt 61
FK 6725 182, 183
Flamingo 176
Fleeze 260
FlowerPot 147
FNP 178
Ford, Henry 135
Fornasetti, Barnaba 96
Fornasetti, Piero 96
Frankfurt Kitchen 237
Frederick, Christine 237
Freud, Sigmund 41
Fritsch, Willy 28
Fritz Hansen 61, 198
Fuchsberger, Joachim 24

G
Garbo, Greta 18
Gatti, Piero 240
Gavina 144
Gerke, Gilian 229
Giudici, Battista 35
Giudici, Gino 35
Goodyear, A. Conger 161
Grant, Hugh 71
Gräshoppa 18
Gray, Eileen 114, 154
Gropius, Walter 24, 111, 205
Grossman, Billy 18
Grossman, Greta 18
G-type 166
Gubi 18
Gufram 65
Gugelot, Hans 242
Guggenheim Museum 91
Guhl, Willy 21
Gursky, Andreas 45

H
Haeusler, Helene 184
Hakusan Porcelain Company 166
Haller, Fritz 102
Hamborg, Mia 138
Hancock, John 130
Harper, Irving 10, 84
Harry, Duke of Sussex 123
Hathaway, Anne 69
Haussmann, Robert 21
Hay 190, 249
Hayon, Jaime 36
HB-Werkstätten 253
Heide, Rolf 220
Heine, Heinrich 76
Helvetica 153
Hemmets forskningsinstitut 109
Henningsen, Agnes 125
Henningsen, Poul 125, 255
Hepburn, Audrey 259
Herkner, Sebastian 26, 45
Herman Miller 84, 119
Hermès 161
Hesser, Petra 121
Hiéronimus, Annie 148
Hildinger, Paul 242
Hilfling 222
Hollande, François 95
Holmblad, Peter 56
Holst & Knudsen 222
Horten 117
Horzon, Rafael 121
Hot Bertaa 192
House of Finn Juhl 74
Howard Miller Clock Company 10
Howard, Vivian 143
Hugo, Victor 76

I
Ibsen, Henrik 48
Iglesias, Enrique 24
Iittala 190, 195
Ikea 87, 99, 121
Immendorff, Jörg 36
Ingeborg 234
iPod 205
Isola, Maija 39
Ive, Jonathan 204

J
Jacobsen, Arne 55, 119, 126, 147, 196, 206, 220, 234, 242
James, Edward 63
Jeanneret-Gris, Charles-Édouard 203
Jeanneret, Pierre 202
Jobs, Steve 204
Johnston, Herbert 132
Jolie, Angelina 12
Jongerius, Hella 17, 250
Juhl, Finn 74, 147, 183
Juicy Salif 123, 192
Junghans 231
Jürgens, Udo 201

K
Kaendler, Johann Joachim 36
Kaiser & Co. 61
Kaiser Idell 6631 61
Karhula-Iittala 195
Karlweis, Oskar 28
Kartell 201
Kastholm, Jørgen 183
Kaufman, James C. 86
Kawazoe Seizan 141
Keaton, Diane 12
Kennedy, John F. 41, 231
Kiefer, Anselm 125
Kill, Alfred 183
King, Martin Luther 240
Kippenberger, Martin 91
KitchenAid 132
Klitschko, Vitali 247
Klitschko, Vladimir 247
KLM 251
Klubben 190
Knoblauch, Walter 169
Knoll International 111, 112, 144
Knotted Chair 107
Koivisto, Eero 229
Kondo, Marie 137
König Alfonso 111
Königin Victoria 111
Kristall 176
Kubrick, Stanley 128

Kubus 79
Kufus, Axel 178
Kuramata, Shiro 176
Kusama, Yayoi 41

L
Laccio 144
La Conica 82
La Cupola 82
Lagerfeld, Karl 55, 176
Lamborghini 88
Lampert, Richard 117
Lamy 2000 130
Lamy, Carl Josef 130
Lamy, Manfred 130
Landels, Willie 218
Lang, Sebastian 172
Lassen, Flemming 233
Lassen, Mogens 79, 234
Lassen, Søren 79
LC4 Chaise Lounge 202
LC4 CP 203
Le Corbusier 111, 154, 202, 203, 255
Le Creuset Cookware 143
Lego 102
Leigh Hunt, James Henry 227
Lennon, John 216
Lido 35
Ligne Roset 148, 216
Liljedahl, Billy 121
Linea Zero 220
Lomazzi, Paolo 43, 99, 218, 219, 240
Loop Chair 21
Louis Vuitton 161, 203
Lounge Chair 92
Louvre 171
Lubs, Dietrich 51
Lucas, George 114
Lucellino 137
Lundgren, Gillis 121
Luti, Lorenza 12
Luxembourg chair 76
Lyngby Porcelæn 222
Lyngby Vase 222

M
Maar, Paul 48
Macy's 241
Madonna 143
Magnussen, Eric 55
Mahal, Mumtaz 96
Mainzer, Philipp 100
Maly 216
Mann, Thomas 81
Margaret, Countess of Snowdon 218
Marguerre, Eva 92
Mari, Enzo 91

Marimekko 39
Marshmallow Sofa 84
Maserati 88
Maurer, Ingo 52, 137
McCartney, Stella 45
McKenzie, Scott 147
Meghan, Duchess of Sussex 123
Melt 31
Memphis 176, 192
Mendelsohn, Erich 117
Merkel, Angela 71
Mer, Yael 92
Mies van der Rohe, Ludwig 87, 111, 112, 225
Minogue, Kylie 65
Miyake, Issey 15
Moeckl, Ernst 172
Mogensen, Børge 147
Molar Stool 100
Monkey (Side table) 36
Monkey (Toy) 47, 184
Mono 256
Mono A 256
Mono Zeug 256
Monroe, Marilyn 143, 231
Mori, Masahiro 166
Moroso 157
Moroso, Patrizia 45, 265
Morrison, Jasper 245
Mouille, Serge 71
Mourgue, Olivier 128
MR 20 225
Müller, Gerd A. 130
Müller, Konrad Rufus 245
Müller, Renate 184
Murch, Walter 114
Museum of Modern Art 22, 104, 119, 150, 161, 171, 186, 205, 231
Museum Ostwall 91
Museum Plagiarius 161
Muuto 190

N
Nadolny, Sten 245
National Museum of Modern Art 166
Nelson, George 10, 84, 128
Nerbel, Martin 71
Neri & Hu 92
Nesting Tables 227
Newman, Paul 231
Nicholson, Jack 182
Nielsen, Holger 169
Nielsen, Jette 171
Nixdorf 172
Nixon, Richard 41
Noguchi, Isamu 161
Norman, Chris 254
Norway Says 190

Nygren, Joakim 229

O
Oda 45
Ólafsson, Sigurjón 74
Ono, Yoko 216
Opperman, Josh 206
Opsvik, Peter 190
Ordrupgaard Art Museum 74

P
Pack 233
Palissade 247
Panton Chair 147, 175, 220
Panton, Verner 147, 242
Paolini, Cesare 240
Paris Parks Department 77
Parupu 229
Pauchard, Xavier 28, 29
Peck, Gregory 259
Pelican 74
Perriand, Charlotte 111, 202, 203, 213, 214
Perry, Katy 65
Perry, Matthew 213
Pestel 175
Pestel, Liv 175
Petersdorff-Campen, Stephan von 144
Petrolchemisches Kombinat Schwedt 172
Pfeiffer, Albert 112
PH 5 126
Piaggio, Enrico 259
Pirandello 245
Pirandello, Luigi 245
Plastic Chair 119
Plumy 148
Pocket radio T3 205
Poeten 74
Polar 176
Polder 250
Pompidou 210
Ponti, Giovanni 88
Pony 220
„Porca Miseria!" 52
Portman, Richard 114
Poulsen, Louis 242
Prada 161
Presley, Elvis 58
Proust, Marcel 240
Puppy 220

R
Raacke, Peter 256
Race, Ernest 209
Radcliffe, Daniel 12
Rams, Dieter 51, 205
Rankin 65
Ratia, Armi 39

R & Company 184
Redford, Robert 254
Reich, Lilly 111, 112
Reidemeister, Kurt 107
Relling, Ingmar 189
Relling, Knut 190
Rice, Jackie 210
Richter, Gerhard 196
Robsjohn-Gibbings, T. H. 161
Rollei 172
Rosendahl Design Group 222
Rosenthal, Philip 24
Roset, Michel 216
Rossi, Aldo 82
Rubens 227
Ruegenberg, Sergius 225
Rühmann, Heinz 28
Rune, Ola 229
Rupfentiere 184

S
S 33 225
S 64 225
Saarinen, Eero 128
Sacco 240
Saint Laurent, Yves 259
Sakakura, Junzo 214
Sapper, Richard 256
SAS Hotel 196, 206
Sato, Oki 15
Savoy vase 195
Schärer, Paul 102
Schmidt, Harald 121
Schmidt, Helmut 245
Schneider, Michael 256
Schocken Department Store 117
Scholten, Stefan 92
Schreibtisch E1 114
Schreibtisch E2 117, 220
Schumacher, Mick 55
Schütte-Lihotzky, Margarete 237
Sciangai 43
Scolari, Carla 218, 219
SD 141
Seibel, Wilhelm 256
Septima 126
Series 7 196
Shah Jahan, Shihabuddin Muhammad 96
Shell Chair 41
Shuffle Table MH1 138
Siesta Chair 189
Simple Minds 254
Sinatra, Frank 58
Snoopy 86, 145
Sottsass, Ettore 176
Spitzweg, Carl 74, 245

Stam, Mart 144, 225, 255
Stanislawski, Konstantin 182
Starck, Philippe 123, 192
Steilmann 81
Steinmeier, Frank-Walter 245
Stelton 55
Stendig 150
Stevenson, Robert Louis 265
Stewart, Ian 79
Stokke 190
Strasberg, Lee 182
Streep, Meryl 182
String Shelf 109, 111
Strinning, Kajsa 109, 111
Strinning, Nils 109, 111
Studio 65 63
Superleggera 88
Swan Chair 196, 206
Sybille shelving system 175

T
Tableware 137, 253
Tac 01 24
Taccia lamp 87
Taj Mahal 96
Taylor, Elizabeth 58, 231
Tea Trolley 901 17
Tecta 144
Teodoro, Franco 240
Tew, Alex 206
The Chair 41
The Tired Man 233
Thomsen, Mette 206
Thonet 111, 114, 144, 202, 225, 255
Thonet coffee shop chair 255
Thonet, Michael 255
Thonet, Peter 255
Thonet, Philipp 255
Thoreau, Henry David 137
Thun, Matteo 176
Tivoli 126
Tolix Stool 29
Tolkien, J. R. R. 265
Totzek, Winfried 260
Toucan 220
Toulouse-Lautrec, Henri de 265
Trigema 81
Tripp Trapp 190
Tube Light 154
Tulip Table 128

U
Ulm Stool 214, 242
Unikko 39
Uno, la mela 91
Urquiola, Patricia 157
USM Haller 102

Uten.Silo 137

V
Venini 66
Vespa 259
Viard, Virginie 55
Vignelli, Massimo 150
Villani, Cédric 79
Vipp 169
Vipp Shelter 171
Vitra 84, 119, 137, 147, 164
Vitra Design Museum 10, 87
Vivienne Westwood 259

W
Wanders, Marcel 107
Wassily Chair 144
Waves 195
Wayne, John 58
Wegner, Hans J. 41, 114, 119, 147, 190
Weißenhof Chair 112
Weissenhof Siedlung 225, 255
Werner, Christian 254
Westnofa 190
Wieland, Adam 117
Wilder, Billy 95
William, Duke of Cambridge 123, 231
Williams, Serena 247
Williams, Venus 247
Winfrey, Oprah 210
Winslet, Kate 69
Wintour, Anna 182
Wirkkala, Tapio 26, 66
Wishbone Chair 41
Woodward, Joanne 231
Wristwatch 231

Y
Yanagi, Sori 213

Z
Zanotta 43, 241
Zanotta, Aurelio 218, 241
Zavater, Alessandro 220
Zettel'z 52, 137
Zola, Emile 240
Z.Stuhl 172
Zyklus 216

PICTURE CREDITS

Cover: GUBI PR

p. 1 Lyngby Porcelain, p. 3 Lyngby Porcelain, p. 11 Ball Clock Design George Nelson, 1948 Vitra Collections AG, p. 13 top: Valerio Castelli/Kartell, p. 13 bottom: Kartell, p. 14 top: Masayuki_Hayashi (3), Illustration: nendo.jp, photo: ddp images, p. 16 Suvi Kesäläinen/artek.fi, p. 17 artek.fi, p. 19 GUBI PR, p. 20 @eternit (Schweiz) AG, p. 22-23 @eternit (Schweiz) AG, p. 25, 26, 27 Rosenthal GmbH, p. 28-29 tolix.fr, p. 30 Pete Navey/Tom Dixon, p. 33 Pete Navey/Tom Dixon, p. 34-35 wb form ag, p. 36 Jaime Hayon/BD Barcelona, p. 37 Nienke Klunder/Jaime Hayon/BD Barcelona, p. 38 Marimekko, p. 40 Carl Hansen & Søn, p. 42 Courtesy of Zanotta SpA, Italy, p. 44, 45 PulpoProducts.com, p. 46-47, 49 Kay Bojesen Denmark, p. 50 Zeon Ltd PR, p. 53 Ingo Maurer GmbH, p. 54-57 Stelton, p. 58, 59 sillaacapulco.com, p. 60 Nicklas Ingemann/Fritz Hansen, p. 61 Fritz Hansen, p. 62-64 Courtesy of Gufram, p. 67 Venini, p. 68 Carl Bergman, 2016 /Duotune/Eero Aarnio, p. 69 Courtesy of Eero Aarnio, p. 70-71, 72, 73 Editions Serge Mouille, p. 75 The Poet Sofa by House of Finn Juhl – Black Sun artwork by Søren Solkær, p. 76-77 Fermob PR, p. 78, 79 by Lassen, p. 80, 81 Embru-Werke AG Schweiz, p. 82, 83 Courtesy of Alessi, p. 85 Vitra Design Museum, photo: Jürgen Hans, p. 86,87 Courtesy of Flos, p. 89 Vitra Design Museum, photo: Jürgen Hans, p. 90 Courtesy of Danese Milano, p. 92-93 Lounge Chair with Ottoman_Totale_Original Campaign_spplmnt © unknown, p. 94-95 Eames Office, LLC eamesoffice.com , p. 96 Courtesy Fornasetti, p. 97 Courtesy Fornasetti (4), photo with Piero Fornasetti: Franco Petazzi, p. 98 Inter IKEA Systems B.V. 2015, p. 101 E15/PHILIPP MAINZER, p.103, 105 USM, p. 106 Marcel Wanders Studio 1996, p. 108 top: Marcus Lawett /String Furniture, bottom: Bruno Ehrs, Freddy Billquist/String Furniture, p. 110 Gionata Xerra/Courtesy of Knoll, p. 112, 113 Courtesy of Knoll, p. 114, 115, 116, 117 Richard Lampert, p. 118 Gilbert Ebrahimi/unsplash, p. 119 Eames Fiberglass Side Chair DSR by Charles & Ray Eames © Vitra, p. 120 Inter IKEA Systems B.V., p. 122 Courtesy of Alessi, p. 124 Louis Poulsen, p. 127 Louis Poulsen, p. 129 Karl Andersen/living4media, Top Foto/mauritius images, Red Cover/Photoshot/Mel Yates/picture alliance, p. 131 Lamy PR, p. 133 Deva Williamson/unsplash, p. 134, 135 KitchenAid, p. 136 Uten.Silo Classic Tray International Love Heart Trays © Vitra International AG, p. 138, 139 Shuffle MH1, in the colour Array, by Mia Hamborg for &Tradition, p. 140 Gerhardt Kellermann (2), DIEZOFFICE (2), p. 142-143 2022, Le Creuset, p. 144 Courtesy of Knoll, p. 145 Santi Caleca/Knoll, p. 146 FlowerPot by Verner Panton © Verner Panton Design AG, &Tradition, p. 148 LIGNE ROSET, p. 149 LIGNE ROSET, p. 150-151 Veerle Evens/Stendig Calendars, p. 152, 153 Veerle Evens/Stendig Calendars, p. 155 ClassiCon / Mark Seelen, Hersteller ClassiCon autorisiert von The World Licence Holder Aram Designs Ltd., p. 156 Courtesy of Patricia Urquiola, p. 158 Allessandro Paderni, p. 159 top: Courtesy of Patricia Urquiola, p. 159 bottom: Alberto Bernasconi/laif, p. 160 Noguchi Coffee Table by Isamu Noguchi – © Vitra, p. 162, 163 Eames Elephant (small) palm green group_F by Charles & Ray Eames – © Vitra, p. 164 Eames Elephant (small) Eames House Bird (white) © Vitra, p. 165 Eames Elephant (Plywood) by Charles & Ray Eames © Vitra International AG, p. 167 Mori Masahiro Design Studio, LLC, p. 168, 169, 170, 171 VIPP A/S vipp.com, p. 173, 174 z.stuhl/Pestel, p. 177 Pariano Angelantonio/Courtesy Memphis Srl/memphis-milano.com, p. 178 Jaeger&Jaeger/FNP, p. 179 Julia Rotter/FNP, p. 180-181 POPO GmbH, Bremen/FNP Museum Weserburg, p. 182 Walter Knoll, p. 184 zb/dpa/picture-alliance, p. 185, 187 ZB/picture-alliance, p. 188 Kristin Stoylen/LK Hjelle, p. 189 Courtesy of LK Hjelle, p. 190 Courtesy of LK Hjelle, p. 191 Kristin Stoylen/LK Hjelle, p. 193 ArtDirectors&TRIP/Alamy Stock Photos/mauritius images, p. 194 Courtesy auf littala, p. 195 Timo Junttila/littala, p. 197 Polly Wreford/Narratives/plainpicture.com, p. 198 1958 SAS Royal Hotel Egg, Swan and Drop by Arne Jacobsen/Courtesy of Fritz Hansen, p. 199 Archivio GBB/Alamy Stock Photos/mauritius images, p. 200 Teixera Rui-Studio Ghigliere/Kartell, p. 202 Pierre Olivier Deschamps/VU/laif, imago/Arcaid Images, p. 204 Apple, p. 205 RetroAdArchives/Alamy Stock Photos/mauritius images, p. 206, 207 designletters.de, p. 208 Race Furniture Classic Collection/racefurniture.com, p. 211 Jonathan Adler, p. 212-213 Butterfly Stool by Sori Yanagi © Vitra, p. 214 Butterfly Stool by Sori Yanagi © Vitra, p. 215 Butterfly Stool by Sori Yanagi, Elliptical Table ETR by Charles & Ray Eames © Vitra, p. 217 LIGNE ROSET, p. 218-219 Courtesy of Zanotta SpA, Italy, p. 221 Linea Zero, p. 222 Lyngby Porcelain, p. 224 Thonet GmbH (2), Michael Gerlach/Thonet GmbH, p. 226 Tony Cenicola/NYT/Redux/laif, p. 228 Denise Grünstein 2008, p. 230, 231 Junghans, p. 232, 233, 234 by Lassen, p. 236, 238, 239 Simon Keckeisen, p. 240, 241 Courtesy of Zanotta SpA, Italy, p. 242, 243 wb form ag, p. 244 Glas Italia/glasitalia.com, p. 246, 247, 248, 249 HAY, p. 250 Marc Eggimann/Vitra, p. 252 Hedwig Bollhagen, p. 254 Constantin Meyer/Thonet GmbH, p. 255 Stephan Abry, p. 256 Michael Schneider, p. 257 Fabian Frinzel/Michael Schneider, p. 258 Lorenzo Gerosa/unsplash, p. 261, 262-263 de Sede AG, p. 264 Courtesy of moroso.it, p. 271 © private

THE AUTHOR

Silke Pfersdorf, born in Hanover in 1963, is a long-time journalist, columnist and book author and regularly publishes in major German magazines and newspapers such as *Brigitte*, *Stern*, *Madame*, *Cosmopolitan*, *DU-Schweizer Kulturmagazin*, *Elle Decoration*, *Geo Saison*, *Süddeutsche Zeitung* and many others. She learned to love Italian design during her studies in Florence and Japanese purism during her years in Tokyo, where she conducted many interviews in the creative scene there. She is known, among other things, for her column „Schätzchen, wo kommst du denn her?" („Sweetheart, where did you come from?") in *Living at home*, in which she highlights a design classic every month. Silke Pfersdorf is a mother of two now grown-up children and lives in Hamburg.

© 2022 teNeues Verlag GmbH

Texts: © Silke Pfersdorf. All rights reserved.
Idea, Concept and Editorial Coordination
by Berrit Barlet, teNeues Verlag
Translations by Heather Bock, WeSwitch Languages
Design by Eva Stadler
Photo Editing by Heide Christiansen
Production by Sandra Jansen-Dorn, teNeues Verlag
Color Separation by Jens Grundei, teNeues Verlag

Typeface of book title and headlines: Magnet by Inga Plönnigs

ISBN: 978-3-96171-417-9
Library of Congress Number: 2022941408

Printed in Slovakia by Neografia

Picture and text rights reserved for all countries. No part of this publication may be reproduced in any manner whatsoever.

While we strive for utmost precision in every detail, we cannot be held responsible for any inaccuracies, neither for any subsequent loss or damage arising.

Every effort has been made by the publisher to contact holders of copyright to obtain permission to reproduce copyrighted material. However, if any permissions have been inadvertently overlooked, teNeues Publishing Group will be pleased to make the necessary and reasonable arrangements at the first opportunity.

Bibliographic information published by the Deutsche Nationalbibliothek: The Deutsche Nationalbibliothek lists this publication in the Deutsche Nationalbibliografie; detailed bibliographic data are available on the Internet at dnb.dnb.de.

Published by teNeues Publishing Group

teNeues Verlag GmbH
Ohmstraße 8a
86199 Augsburg, Germany

Düsseldorf Office
Waldenburger Str. 13, 41564 Kaarst, Germany
Email: books@teneues.com

Augsburg/Munich Office
Ohmstraße 8a
86199 Augsburg, Germany
Email: books@teneues.com

Berlin Office
Lietzenburger Str. 53, 10719 Berlin, Germany
Email: books@teneues.com

Press Department: Stefan Becht
Phone: +49-152-2874-9508 /
+49-6321-97067-97
Email: sbecht@teneues.com

teNeues Publishing Company
350 Seventh Avenue, Suite 301, New York,
NY 10001, USA

www.teneues.com

teNeues Publishing Group
Augsburg / München
Berlin
Düsseldorf
London
New York

teNeues